THE
SHORTEST
HISTORY
OF
JAPAN

From Mythological Origins to Pop Culture Powerhouse—The Global Drama of an Ancient Island Nation

LESLEY DOWNER

THE EXPERIMENT

NEW YORK

The Experiment, LLC
220 East 23rd Street, Suite 600
New York, NY 10010-4658
theexperimentpublishing.com

THE EXPERIMENT and its colophon are registered trademarks of The Experiment, LLC. Many of the designations used by manufacturers and sellers to distinguish their products are claimed as trademarks. Where those designations appear in this book and The Experiment was aware of a trademark claim, the designations have been capitalized.

The Experiment's books are available at special discounts when purchased in bulk for premiums and sales promotions as well as for fundraising or educational use. For details, contact us at info@theexperimentpublishing.com.

Library of Congress Cataloging-in-Publication Data

Names: Downer, Lesley, author.
Title: The shortest history of Japan : from mythical origins to pop culture powerhouse, the global drama of an ancient island nation / Lesley Downer.
Description: New York : The Experiment, 2024. | Originally published in Australia by Black Inc. First published in revised form in North America by The Experiment, LLC.--Galley. | Includes bibliographical references and index.
Identifiers: LCCN 2024022166 (print) | LCCN 2024022167 (ebook) | ISBN 9781891011665 (paperback) | ISBN 9781891011672 (ebook)
Subjects: LCSH: Japan--History.
Classification: LCC DS806 .D696 2024 (print) | LCC DS806 (ebook) | DDC 952--dc23/eng/20240516
LC record available at https://lccn.loc.gov/2024022166
LC ebook record available at https://lccn.loc.gov/2024022167

ISBN 978-1-891011-66-5
Ebook ISBN 978-1-891011-67-2

Cover and text design by Jack Dunnington

Manufactured in the United States of America

First printing July 2024
10 9 8 7 6 5 4 3 2 1

In memory of my Chinese-Canadian mum, Lily Chan,
and my Canadian Sinophile dad, Gordon Downer.
And to Arthur, who, as always, shared this journey with me.

Contents

RUSSIA

HOKKAIDO

○ Sapporo

○ Hakodate

○ Aomori

○ Morioka

Sea of Japan

Sendai

Niigata

○ Fukushima

SNOW COUNTRY

HONSHU

JAPAN ALPS

Kanazawa ○

Tokyo

Yokohama ○

Mount Fuji ▲

Kamakura

L. Biwa

○ Nagoya

Kyoto ○

Izu Peninsula

Kobe ○ ○ Osaka

Hiroshima ○

SHIKOKU

PACIFIC OCEAN

Fukuoka

KYUSHU

Nagasaki ○

Kagoshima ○

N

0 ___ 200 km

0 ___ 200 miles

Japan

List of Maps

Chronology

PALEOLITHIC/ NEOLITHIC (14,500–100 BCE)	**JŌMON (14,500–100 BCE)**	Legendary founding of Japan by Emperor Jimmu (February 11, 660 BCE)
		Jōmon culture
ANCIENT JAPAN (300 BCE–710 BCE)	**YAYOI (300 BCE–300 CE)**	Iron Age and rice cultivation arrive from China by way of Korea
		First settlements, first wars
		Queen Himiko (168–248 CE)
	Kofun period (300–538 CE)	Burial mounds (kofun)
	Asuka period (538–710)	Rise of the Yamato clan
		Writing and Buddhism arrive from China by way of Korea
		Advent of the emperor
CLASSICAL JAPAN (710–1180)	**Nara period (710–794)**	Cultural exchange with China and along Silk Road
		Building of Hōryūji and Great Buddha
		First written history and literature: Kojiki, Nihon Shoki, Manyōshū
	Heian period (794–1180)	Expanding the empire
		Golden Age of peace
		Tale of Genji (1008)
		Byōdōin (Phoenix Hall)

SHOGUNAL RULE (1180–1868)	**Kamakura period (1180–1333)**	Battle of Ichi no Tani (1184)
		Battle of Dan no ura (1185)
		Tale of the Heiki
		Mongol invasions (1274, 1281)
	Muromachi period (1333–1573)	Kinkakuji (Golden Pavilion)
		Birth of Nōh theater
		Development of tea ceremony, ink painting, and other Japanese arts
		Portuguese arrive, bringing guns (1543)
	Azuchi Momoyama period (1573–1603)	"Christian century"
		"Country at war"
		Momoyama period of extravagant arts
	Edo period (1603–1853)	Battle of Sekigahara (1603)
		Tokugawa Renaissance
		Pleasure quarter culture
		Utamaro (1753–1806) and Hokusai (1760–1849) creating woodblock prints
	Bakumatsu: Fall of the Tokugawa shogunate (1853–1868)	"Black Ships" sail into Edo Bay
		Meiji "Restoration"
MODERN JAPAN (1868–PRESENT)	**Meiji period (1868–1912)**	Meiji reforms, rapid modernization
		Taking Hokkaido, Okinawa, Korea
		Sino-Japanese War (1895)
		Russo-Japanese War (1905)
	Taishō period (1912–1926)	Jazz Age
		Great Earthquake (1923)
	Shōwa period (1926–1989)	World War II (1939–1945)
		American Occupation
		Tokyo Olympics (1964)
		"Bubble economy"
	Heisei period (1989–2019)	Fukushima (2011)
	Reiwa period (2019–present)	Tokyo Olympics 2020 (held in 2021)
		Dispute over South China Sea

The Land of Wa: Japan from Jōmon to Heian

Introduction
Before Time Began

AGE OF THE GODS

The story of Japan begins with a dance.

In the beginning, there was chaos. Then deities emerged from the primordial ooze, and after seven generations two brother and sister gods, Izanagi and Izanami, were born. Commanded by the older gods to form order from the chaos, they descended from heaven on a rainbow bridge. Izanagi dipped his spear in the oily primordial mass and drops fell from its tip and formed the islands of Japan.

Myriads of other gods emerged from the loins of these two. One was Amaterasu, the Sun Goddess. While she was happy, there was light. But one day, her brother, the Storm God, insulted her and she hid in a cave, plunging the world into darkness. The gods thought up ways to lure her out, but nothing worked. Finally, the Goddess of Dance and Merriment broke into an exuberant and distinctly unseemly dance, tearing off her clothes. The gods burst into uproarious laughter and Amaterasu, unable to contain her curiosity, peeked out of her cave. And so the world was saved.

THE JŌMON, HUNTER-GATHERERS IN A LAND OF PLENTY

It is 14,500 BCE. Dawn in a forest, somewhere on the eastern edge of the Asian continent, deep in the mists of time. People are gathering wood while others kneel, making a bonfire. They shiver and pull their animal-skin coats more closely around their thin, woven garments. Some wear their long hair loose, others have it tied in place with bone or wooden hairpins.

They've discovered that where they make bonfires the earth beneath is burnt rock hard. The clay soil is dense and malleable. A woman takes a handful and shapes it, fashioning a hollow with her thumb, squeezing the edges into walls, easing them out, making them thinner.

Spectacular flame pots, made between 3500 and 2500 BCE, were used for cooking and storage, but the creators also enjoyed the decorative possibilities. The rope designs were originally modeled on woven baskets and may have had specific symbolic meanings.

Then she puts her molded clay into the fire. It comes out hard, impermeable enough to hold water or food. It's a pot, a revolutionary new technology that will transform all their lives. Millennia later, she and her people will come to be called *Jō-mon*, "rope design," after the twisted cord patterns that they impress on their pots.

The first Jōmon pots have been carbon dated to 14,500 BCE. In the West, it would be another seven thousand years before Mesopotamians were making their first pots and many more centuries before the Sphinx or the pyramids were constructed. But in Japan and China, millennia before others started making pots anywhere else in the world, people were boiling and storing their food.

Long before the Jōmon started making pots, the world was engulfed in the Ice Age. Much ocean water had frozen and sea levels fell so low that great tracts of land, called "land bridges," joined the Asian mainland—present-day Siberia and Korea—to what is now Japan. People who would become the ancestors of the Jōmon trekked eastward toward the sun, following herds of long-tusked prehistoric elephants and giant deer, in search of game to hunt and food to forage.

It was cold and snowy and there were terrible storms. Food was hard to find. But once the Jōmon had pots, they boiled vegetables, acorns, and horse chestnuts and carried supplies with them when they traveled. They cooked soft food for babies and toothless old people, who could live longer and pass on their lore.

Around 11,000 BCE, the glaciers melted. The ice retreated and the seas rose and severed the land bridges, creating the islands that we know as Japan. The weather became balmy, warm, and humid with plenty of rainfall.

These hunter-gatherers found themselves in a land of plenty, a kind of paradise. There were nuts, berries, roots, fruits, seeds, and mushrooms to be gathered in the lush deciduous forests that covered the hillsides; and wild boar, deer, mountain goats, and bears to be hunted, trapped, or chased down with dogs. Higher up the slopes, the hunters found obsidian, hard volcanic rock that they chipped into arrowheads and spear tips. Where the land bridges had been were shallow seas teeming with tuna, porpoises, seals, and salmon. They dined on shellfish, crabs, and seaweed, leaving enormous refuse heaps of shells.

The land was so fertile that they didn't need to roam far in search of food. Most hunter-gatherers didn't make pottery, which would have been heavy to lug around. But these settled down and over time developed a rich and sophisticated culture. Little by little, the population grew from a few thousand to a quarter of a million.

Ten thousand years after that first pot, around 4000 BCE, they began to form communities. They built houses with thick thatch that stretched to the ground and a pit in the center where a fire crackled, sending smoke billowing out of a circular opening in the roof. Besides foraging, people cultivated soybeans, gourds, hemp, aduki beans, and peaches.

A particularly large community grew up at Sannai Maruyama in the north of Honshu island. By 2900 BCE, there were seven hundred houses, some with stone floors, with thatched storage houses on stilts for food and watchtowers on massive wooden pillars. There were other settlements too, mainly in Honshu and Kyushu. At the center of many were oval longhouses, great halls where people from all around met for rituals and festivals. Some became potters, making magnificent pots with exuberant wave and flame designs leaping around the flared rims, which they used for cooking and serving. Every pot was different, and each was a work of art; this was a society that appreciated artistry.

Some of the artisans made *dogū* ("earth spirits"), beautifully crafted figurines, some with bulging eyes and elaborate hairstyles or pregnant like earth mothers, others in the shape of dogs or pigs.

The *dogū* help us imagine the Jōmon and their lives. We picture them in their longhouses, their faces and bodies tattooed, in garments woven from

Dogū *created in the Final Jōmon period (1000–300 BCE), in Kamegaoka, near Sannai Maruyama. It is hollow inside and was carefully burnished before it was fired. It was originally painted with red pigment and traces can still be seen.*

mulberry bark or hemp, wearing earrings, necklaces, and pendants. Many are missing teeth, deliberately knocked out as a rite of passage. They dance and sing to the music of drums, zithers, and deer-antler whistles and gather while shamans who have consumed mushrooms or alcohol enter trances and mediate with the spirits to request success in their fishing and hunting trips and protection against eruptions, typhoons, floods, and earthquakes.

Sannai Maruyama was a major trading center. People trekked from village to village or shuttled in dugout canoes across the straits to Ezo, now Hokkaido, or even to mainland Asia. They traded obsidian arrowheads, lacquerware, pottery, jade, amber, salt, shell bracelets, bone and antler needles, fishhooks, and toggle-head harpoons.

But then around 1500 BCE the climate started to cool. Nevertheless, when farmers began to settle on the island of Kyushu, sculling across from the Korean peninsula around 900 BCE, the Jōmon did not follow their example and take up farming. Why should they break their backs hoeing and tilling when they could still gather as much food as they needed?

The climate grew still cooler and food became less abundant and the Jōmon population declined rather sharply. Huge changes were about to begin.

AT THE EDGE OF THE WORLD

The lives of the Jōmon and all those who followed them were intimately bound up with the land they lived in.

Japan is a country of islands, strung like a necklace around the Asian mainland, from Korea in the south to Siberia in the north. Even at the nearest point, it's still about 120 miles

(190 km) from mainland Asia, a lot further than Britain is from Europe, and considerably more remote. The sea provides an effective barrier against invasion and has enabled the culture to develop in unique and distinctive ways. It has also meant that at crucial times the Japanese have been able to isolate themselves from developments elsewhere in the world.

Throughout its history, Japan has had a complicated relationship with its neighbors, Korea and China. For many centuries, China was to the rest of Asia as Greece and Rome were to Europe, a beacon of civilization, setting a pattern that others followed. The early Japanese borrowed much of their art, philosophy, religion, and even writing from China, then transmuted them to create a unique culture.

The Japanese archipelago is long and narrow. It stretches nearly 2,000 miles (3,200 km), with huge variations of climate and landscape, from Hokkaido in the north, buried under snow for nearly half the year, to subtropical Okinawa in the south. From east to west, you are never very far from the sea.

Four-fifths of the land is densely forested mountains, leaving very little flat land for settlement or agriculture. The coastal plains, where most of the population lives, are extraordinarily fertile. In central and southern Japan, a huge amount of rain falls. In the hot humid summers, you can almost see rice plants sprouting and bamboo shoots surging up.

The land is geologically young, studded with active volcanoes. It's a landscape in upheaval. Earthquakes crack open the ground, making it undulate like an ocean, and there are eruptions and tidal waves. Hot water reeking of sulfur gushes from fissures in the rocks. Tremors are part of everyday life.

The Jōmon would have experienced their world crashing down around them, not as a rare occurrence but as something known and feared. There would have been good reason to believe there were spirits in nature whom it would make sense to propitiate.

Many early peoples worshipped nature. But while in other cultures this early animistic belief faded away or was absorbed into universal faiths such as Buddhism or Christianity, in Japan it remains strong, perhaps because of Japan's isolation and remoteness or perhaps because of the wild capriciousness of nature. Known as Shinto, the way of the gods, it is considered the native Japanese religion, whereas Buddhism is foreign, imported. In Japan, Buddhism and Shinto exist side by side. The Shinto *kami* (gods) are everywhere—the sky, mountains, mountain ranges, trees, and rocks. They take care of you in life; they keep you healthy, help you find love, and ensure your business is successful. Conversely, Buddhism takes care of you after death.

There are regular festivals, Bacchanalian affairs where sweating youths in loincloths carry *mikoshi*, floats bearing the gods, through the streets, chanting, shouting, and consuming copious amounts of sake. The Jōmon probably enjoyed similar festivities.

Often the festivals mark the changes of the seasons. Since ancient times, the Japanese have celebrated their four very distinct seasons—the plum and cherry blossoms in spring, the heat of summer when there is dancing and fireworks, the full moon and brilliantly colored maple leaves in autumn, the snow in winter. This heightened awareness of the surrounding world and of beauty colors Japanese culture, alongside a profound sense of the fleeting nature of all things, including human life. All this has created a very distinctive aesthetic—a love of the rough and natural-looking, the asymmetric, which

Inuyama festival celebrating the flowering of the cherry blossom

we see right from the start in Jōmon pots. It's also expressed in poetry. From the earliest times, Japanese have loved to record their feelings and response to nature and to what life throws their way in poems.

This is the story of a small country at the very edge of the world that managed to avoid colonization, overcome the devastation of World War II, and not just spring back but become immensely successful and prosperous, while maintaining its unique character and culture. It's the story of an emperor descended from the Sun Goddess, of empresses, warlords, samurai, merchants, businessmen, women warriors, court ladies, geisha, and all the larger-than-life individuals who shaped this extraordinary society.

Some key points

- In this book, I've divided the eras in the traditional way, by historical phase, then by where the capital was located, and after 1868 by emperor, using the era name, which also became the emperor's posthumous name.

- The Japanese have an easygoing approach to religion. Buddhist temples and Shinto shrines are often side by side, with a Shinto shrine inside a Buddhist temple. In English, "temple" conventionally indicates a Buddhist place of worship, while "shrine" is a Shinto place of worship.

- I use the Japanese order for names, surname first. People often change their names to mark the different stages of life, like a pen name or a stage name. Famous people are usually referred to by their first name or pen name, as in Basho or Saikaku. Family members often have very similar given names to indicate continuity and connection. I've reduced the number of names I've used, particularly when names are very similar, to avoid confusion.

- In earlier eras, clan name and given name were often linked by *no*, "of." Minamoto no Yoshitsune is Yoshitsune of the Minamoto clan, like Charles de Gaulle or Otto von Habsburg.

- Important people such as emperors have a posthumous name; Meiji is the posthumous name of Emperor Mutsuhito.

- Japanese names and words are generally pronounced as they are spelled, with each syllable distinct. Vowels are pure and consonants non-aspirated, like Italian. There is equal stress on all syllables; Japanese poems are about syllable count rather than rhyme or rhythm.

- The macron indicates where *o* and *u* should be lengthened. I've omitted the macron from commonplace names such as Tokyo and Kyoto and historical terms such as daimyo and shogun.

CHAPTER 1

Children of the Sun

400 BCE–710 CE

THE FIRST EMPEROR

Dissatisfied with the multitudinous deities who had taken over the newly created land of luxuriant rice fields, Amaterasu the Sun Goddess sent her grandson Ninigi down to rule over them. To establish his authority, she gave him the three sacred regalia: a bronze mirror, a sword, and a curved jewel.

Ninigi landed on Mount Takachiho in Kyushu. He took a beautiful goddess, Princess Flowering Blossom, to be his consort, but her father demanded that he take her ugly sister as well. When Ninigi refused, the father cursed their offspring, decreeing that their lives would be "as brief as the cherry blossom." Thus, the race of mortals was born.

Three generations later, Ninigi's great-grandson, Jimmu, battled his way to the center of the country and established his capital there and, on February 11, 660 BCE, founded the empire of Japan.

THE YAYOI: AGRICULTURE BRINGS WEALTH AND WARFARE

In 57 CE, an envoy from a place the Chinese called the Land of Wa—"Dwarf Country" or "Land of Subject People"—made an epic journey by ship, ox cart, and sedan chair to Luoyang, the magnificent capital of the mighty Chinese empire, bearing tribute. Emperor Guangwu of the Later Han Dynasty accepted this distant territory as a tributary and presented the envoy with a solid gold seal, inscribed "to the King of Na in the land of Wa." Amazingly, the small square seal was found in 1784, buried in a field in northern Kyushu. The Chinese record of this visit is the first written reference to the land that would become Japan. It would be another five centuries before the Japanese adopted writing.

While the Jōmon carried on their hunter-gatherer lifestyle, on the Korean peninsula farmers were scratching a living from the soil, growing rice in dry fields. Their great neighbor China had had agriculture, metal tools, and writing for a thousand years, and some of these developments had spread to Korea. But Korea's colder climate made it harder to grow rice.

Eventually, some of these impoverished farmers began to cross the straits to Kyushu. They established settlements and traded with the Jōmon. Kyushu was warmer and swampier than Korea and rice grew better there.

In other parts of the world, hunter-gatherers quickly took up farming. But the prosperous Jōmon didn't need to.

Then, around 400 BCE, life suddenly and dramatically changed. As the Jōmon population declined, Korea's farming population boomed, and waves of immigrants began to arrive in greater numbers than ever before. Some were refugees fleeing the constant warfare in Korea.

The newcomers were taller, more lightly built, and with slenderer faces than the Jōmon. They brought with them bronze and iron tools and began making wooden shovels, hoes, and ploughs and digging and irrigating paddy fields. And thus, the Iron Age arrived.

Like the Jōmon, the newcomers made pots. Theirs were more austere than the Jōmon pots: clean, functional, smooth shapes, fired at higher temperatures to a reddish-brown color. Archaeologists dubbed the new lifestyle Yayoi, after the Tokyo district where their pottery was first discovered in 1884.

The Jōmon also took up rice cultivation, but little by little the newcomers took over. Some intermarried, but eventually the Jōmon remained mainly in the north. The Ainu of Hokkaido are often thought to be their descendants and preserve aspects of their culture, including face tattoos. The Yayoi who came over from Korea went on to populate the archipelago. Most modern-day Japanese are descended from them.

As agriculture developed, people moved from the forests to the fertile plains and formed permanent farming communities. Some drained the paddies to grow millet, barley, and wheat in winter. They introduced many other crops, along with domesticated pigs. All this triggered a population explosion in Kyushu, and from there farming quickly spread across Japan.

The Yayoi lived in wood and stone houses on stilts with thatched roofs. They forged farming tools, weapons, armor, and bronze mirrors with elaborate designs on the back. They also made *dōtaku*, big ceremonial bronze bells.

Agriculture brought trouble. While the prosperous Jōmon had had plenty of food to go round and had been fairly egalitarian, the Yayoi began to hoard their rice. It became a form of wealth. People could trade it, and those who had more had power over those who had less. In this way, a class system developed, with overlords, commoners, and slaves. From about 100 BCE, they started burying their elite in splendid graves, together with luxury goods such as glass beads, jade and bronze swords, and mirrors.

As the population grew, villages grouped together. Hundreds, then thousands of people settled on the plains and on hilltops. By the first century CE, there were more than a hundred small kingdoms. The best swampland and plains suitable for growing rice filled up and there was fighting, then wars, over land and water.

At Yoshinogari, once a huge Yayoi settlement in northern Kyushu, archaeologists discovered stone and bronze weapons, caches of arrowheads, headless skeletons and others with arrowheads embedded in their skulls and limbs. There, 1,200 people once lived, surrounded by a protective moat. Inside were more fortifications, watchtowers and fences with gates, communal kitchens, a meeting house, and an inner enclosure where the ruler lived.

After seed sowing in the fifth month and harvest in the tenth, the Yayoi held festivals where they offered prayers and fermented rice liquor to the gods and the ancestral spirits.

Shamans led the ritual dancing, wearing bronze mirrors that reflected the sun's rays and were perhaps used for divination and magic, marking them out as being in touch with higher powers. From early times, the shamans were all-important in ensuring the well-being of the tribe. It made sense to choose a shaman as ruler, and many of these were women.

Yoshinogari watchtower: The Yayoi lived in a time of wars and needed to watch out for enemies.

HIMIKO, SHAMAN QUEEN

In 238 CE, a diplomatic mission from the land of Wa arrived in the capital of the Chinese Wei dynasty, bringing tribute of four male slaves and six female slaves, plus two rolls of cloth, each 20 feet (6 m) long. The Chinese dynastic chronicles record that the emperor responded: "You live very far away across the sea; yet you have sent an embassy with tribute. Your loyalty and filial piety we appreciate exceedingly. We confer upon you therefore the title 'Queen of Wa Friendly to Wei,' together with the decoration of the gold seal with purple ribbon. We expect you, O Queen, to rule your people in peace and to endeavor to be devoted and obedient." He sent Queen Himiko a gift of a hundred bronze mirrors.

Himiko, "Sun Priestess" or "Daughter of the Sun," is the first name in Japanese history to come floating up through the mists of time, though it's not known whether she really existed or is legendary. There is no mention of her in the *Kojiki* or the *Nihon Shoki*, Japanese histories assembled centuries after her time, but her life is recorded in detail in the Chinese annals contemporary to her.

According to those annals, Himiko was a shaman and a woman of extraordinary powers. In 190 CE, when she was twenty, thirty small kingdoms made a truce after years of civil war, formed a confederation, and chose her to be their queen. The Chinese records say that she came from a long dynasty of female rulers and was a virgin who never married but "occupied herself with magic and sorcery, bewitching the people. Thereupon they placed her on the throne." The Chinese called the land of Wa the Queen Country, a country ruled by queens. Himiko's people called it Yamatai.

Himiko was the mouthpiece of the gods. She represented them on earth and intervened with them to ensure good harvests, prosperity, and peace. To maintain her mystery, she kept hidden. Her palace was surrounded by towers and stockades like the fortifications at Yoshinogari and guarded by a large army. A thousand women attendants waited on her, along with one man who served her food and drink and was her spokesperson.

Himiko established rigorous laws and customs and had them strictly enforced. Under her rule, Yamatai prospered, with a taxation system and thriving trade. Her younger brother was her second-in-command, maintaining diplomatic relations with China.

Himiko ruled for sixty years and died in 248 CE, when she was eighty. She was given a magnificent send-off. "A great mound was raised over her, more than a hundred paces in diameter, and over a hundred male and female attendants followed her in death," say the Chinese records.

After her death, a king took the throne, but the people refused to obey him. There were assassinations and murders. Finally, they chose a thirteen-year-old girl named Iyo, a relative of Himiko. Under this teenage shaman queen, order was restored.

Some say Himiko's land of Yamatai was around Yoshinogari, others that it was the Nara region, soon to become the heart of a unified Japan.

KOFUN PERIOD (250–538 CE): THE RISE OF YAMATO

Outside Nara is a tree-covered hill the shape of a keyhole, a perfectly symmetrical, round tumulus with a triangular extension. It rises steeply out of the paddy fields, bordered on one side by a lake. It's the oldest *kofun* (ancient grave) in Japan. Pottery found inside has been dated to 250 CE, the time of Himiko's death, and scholars think it may be Himiko's tomb.

After Himiko's death, burial mounds began to spring up in the Nara region, across Honshu and eventually down to Kyushu. There are some twenty thousand, built over three hundred years. Many are surrounded by moats. Inside is a burial chamber containing a coffin or coffins, surrounded by treasures—jewels, mirrors,

Terra-cotta haniwa *of a sixth-century warrior in a fitted jacket with a flared skirt, helmet, and sword*

weapons—along with attendants: not living attendants as Himiko had, but *haniwa*, large terra-cotta figures with mask-like faces. Through them we can imagine the variety of people who would have been around at the time. There are warriors in armor, dancers, female shamans holding offering bowls, belted wrestlers, and musicians playing drums, zithers, and bells, along with steep-roofed houses, boats, lovingly crafted horses with manes and bridles, boars, and monkeys, surrounding the dead with familiar artifacts, recreating the world that they came from, and ensuring they would feel at home in the next.

Nintoku's keyhole-shaped tomb covers more ground than the Great Pyramid.

Some of the dead were mounted warriors, buried with their weapons and armor. Their helmets, saddles, and decorative horse trappings are bound with patterned silk and hung with gilded pendants, intriguingly similar to those found in North Asia. There are crowns, bronze shoes, and gold and silver jewelry, and agricultural tools such as hoes and spades. One giant tomb in Kyushu overlooking the sea contains the remains of a queen in her late thirties or forties, with ceremonial mirrors, jewels, swords, spears, and stone axes to mark her status and power. The most spectacular of all, the mausoleum of Nintoku, the legendary sixteenth emperor, must have required years and sophisticated construction techniques to build. These rulers were powerful enough to marshal armies of workers and to be celebrated after death with pomp and splendor.

The country was still filled with warring clans, whose chieftains competed to have more and more grandiose burial mounds. The most powerful were the Yamato, perhaps descendants of Himiko's Yamatai, who lived on the fertile plains around modern-day Nara. They began to subdue other clans, sometimes by conquest, sometimes by giving rival chieftains titles and positions in their administration and thus drawing them into their orbit. The arms and armor they were buried with show they had the military strength to do so. Powerful female shamans paid homage to the gods of rival clans, absorbing them into their pantheon. Thus, the Yamato started to build an empire.

For 150 years after Himiko's death, the Chinese annals contain no reports of the land of Wa. Presumably the people were too busy fighting to send tribute. Then, between 413 and 502, five successive Yamato rulers sent emissaries to the all-powerful Chinese court, petitioning the emperor to recognize their royal status. These rulers called themselves Great Sovereigns. The kingdom of Yamato was now a single state, which stretched from Central Honshu all the way down to Kyushu.

China, with its bureaucratic structure, writing, and philosophical systems, was the supreme power in East Asia. It was the dazzling cultural hub from which outlying countries such as Japan strove to learn. It embodied civilization. On the Korean peninsula, the Three Kingdoms of Silla, Baekje, and Goguryeo were battling for supremacy, and for much of this period there was civil war in China among the Northern and Southern Dynasties. Refugees began to flood into Japan, bringing with them Chinese ideas, culture, technology, and goods.

They also brought Chinese writing and learning. The Yamato court began to use Chinese as its official language.

Chinese became the language of scholarship and the mark of an educated person, like Latin in the West.

Literacy opened up Chinese medicine, the Chinese calendar, astronomy, and Confucianism, and Japanese scholars evolved ways of using Chinese characters to write the very different Japanese language. Horse riding and new ceramic and metallurgical techniques, along with important developments in agriculture, were also imported from the Asian mainland.

Many of the Korean and Chinese settlers were master artisans. The highest-ranking and most talented were given provinces and high positions at court, which helped to strengthen the Great Sovereign's hand against the fractious clans who made up his domain. By the ninth century, a third of the nobility claimed descent from the continent, like William the Conqueror's French nobles.

But the next import from the continent was to be even more epoch-making.

ASUKA PERIOD (538–710 CE): THE BUDDHA MEETS THE *KAMI*

In 538 CE, an embassy arrived from the kingdom of Baekje, one of the three warring Korean kingdoms, requesting military support. The king sent artisans, monks, artifacts, and a momentous gift: a bronze statue of the Buddha, along with ritual banners and a collection of sutras, urging the Great Sovereign to adopt this "most excellent" of doctrines.

The Buddhism that arrived in Japan had traveled along the Silk Roads from India to China and Korea, and was colored by those cultures. Mahayana Buddhism, the Great Vehicle, was far more elaborate and complex than the austere teachings of the historical Buddha, Gautama, and of Theravada

Buddhism, the Lesser Vehicle, which flourished in Ceylon. In the Mahayana tradition, the Buddhas were beings who appeared in human form and were worshipped in temples, and there was a body of doctrine laid out in scriptures.

In fact, the Japanese already had a religion. For them, Japan was the land of the gods. They worshipped the *kami*, the myriad gods who had been born from Izanagi and Izanami and who imbued all of nature. There were gods in the rocks, in trees, in mountains, and they protected families, clans, and whole kingdoms. They had no form and there was no formalized system of worship and no sacred texts. The most important god was the Sun Goddess, Amaterasu.

The Great Sovereign Kinmei was the first historical (as opposed to legendary) ruler of Yamato and is known to history as Emperor Kinmei, though the term *tennō*, "emperor," had not yet come into use. He was under the thumb of his powerful advisers, the Soga and Mononobe families.

The Soga favored reform. They had consolidated their power by marrying their daughters into the imperial family, with the result that most of the rulers were the sons and husbands of Soga women. They were descended from Korean immigrants and saw Buddhism, the religion of China, as the essential foundation stone of a civilized society.

Conversely, the Mononobe and their allies, the Nakatomi family, opposed any change in the system. They made up the elite imperial guard and monopolized the rites and rituals to honor the *kami*. They declared that the *kami* would be angry if the Japanese worshipped foreign gods.

So the emperor decided to test the new religion by authorizing the Soga to perform rituals before the statue. Almost immediately, an epidemic broke out, clear evidence that the *kami* were offended. The Mononobe ordered the statue to be tossed into a canal and had the newly built Buddhist temple burned to the ground and three Buddhist nuns flogged. As if in response, a bolt of lightning destroyed the entire imperial palace, killing those who had thrown away the image.

Eventually, the rival factions clashed in a three-day battle at Mount Shigi in 587. The Soga were driven back. It seemed that Buddhism and its supporters had lost.

Then a thirteen-year-old youth stepped in to turn the tide, not just of the battle, but the course of Japanese history. He cut down a sacred *nuride* tree, carved a tiny image of the Four Buddhist Heavenly Kings out of it, and tied it to his forehead, vowing to build the Heavenly Kings a temple if the Soga were victorious. In the battle that followed, the Mononobe leader was killed. In this way, Buddhism was established as the dominant religion of the court.

The young man's name was Prince Umayado, the Prince of the Stable Door; his mother had given birth to him outside the imperial stables. He was Emperor Kinmei's grandson. He has gone down in history as Prince Shōtoku, "Saintly Virtue," and is revered as the founder of the Japanese state and one of Japan's most brilliant rulers.

The victorious Soga chieftain, now chief minister, appointed artisans from the Korean kingdom of Baekje to oversee the building of Japan's first Buddhist temple, Asuka Temple, with three main halls surrounding a five-story pagoda. The great hall was dominated by an austere bronze Buddha image, stern but tranquil, seated in lotus position, deep in meditation. It was the first Buddha statue ever made in Japan.

*Asuka Buddha, created by Tori Busshi, "Tori the maker of Buddha images,"
the greatest sculptor of his day*

The heart of the Yamato kingdom was the beautiful plain of Asuka, a place of lush paddy fields and gentle hills south of modern-day Nara. There was no fixed capital yet. When an emperor died, the entire court left the palace and built a new one so that the new emperor would not be jinxed by the spirit of his predecessor. The capital moved with the emperors from one place to the next.

After Kinmei's death, his daughter became empress. As the regent, Prince Shōtoku held the reins of power. He was a great statesman, intellectual, and patron of the arts and introduced Chinese culture on a sweeping scale.

In the past, power had been distributed between the clan chieftains. Shōtoku drew up Japan's first constitution on Buddhist and Confucian lines with the emphasis on ethical government and brought in a Chinese-style system of court ranks based on merit. He sent Japan's first official embassy to China, to the newly established Sui dynasty, to study Chinese political systems, Buddhism, and Confucianism. Determined to set Japan on an equal footing with China, he drafted a letter from the empress to the Chinese emperor, addressing it "From the sovereign of the land of the rising sun to the sovereign of the land of the setting sun." The emperor was reportedly furious at such audacity and refused to reply. Shōtoku also wrote two chronicles of Japanese history that formed the basis for later histories of Japan.

As a devout Buddhist, he commissioned more than forty temples, magnificent buildings with splendid interiors and awe-inspiring rituals, robes, incense, and chanting, which made a deep impression on everyone's imagination. Hōryūji, the oldest surviving wooden structure in the world, houses a beautiful statue of Kannon, the Bodhisattva of compassion, gazing down with an expression of unearthly tenderness.

Shōtoku had laid firm foundations. But it took a spectacular coup d'état to bind what was still a confederation of fairly autonomous kingdoms into a unified imperial system.

COUP D'ÉTAT

In 645, Nakatomi no Kamatari met the empress's nineteen-year-old son, Prince Naka, over a game of *kemari*, court kickball. Kamatari was the chieftain of the Nakatomi clan, old allies of the Mononobe who had been defeated by the Soga half a century earlier. Both men hated the Soga, who were now so strongly entrenched that it seemed they would carry on ruling in the name of the imperial family forever. The two started meeting in a wisteria arbor, supposedly to study Chinese texts.

One summer's day, the court assembled for an important ceremony. Prince Naka made sure the palace gates were barred, bribed the guards, and hid a spear in the audience chamber. Then in front of everyone, including the empress, he hacked the young leader of the Soga to pieces. The empress abdicated forthwith, having been defiled by being in the presence of death.

In this way, the imperial family regained political power. Prince Naka made his uncle emperor but held on to power along with his co-conspirator, Nakatomi, to whom he gave the name Fujiwara, "Wisteria Arbor," to commemorate their meetings. He set about instituting a program of reforms known as Taika, "Great Change," giving the emperor absolute power over the land and all its people, including the former clan chieftains, on the basis that "There are not two suns in the sky or two lords on the earth." It was a bloodless revolution. He set up three ministries to advise the throne: the minister of the left (the highest post), the minister of the right, and the minister of the center, the chancellor.

He also introduced a sweeping land reform, taking over all the land and distributing it equally to the farmers, at a stroke removing the powerbases of the clan chieftains and creating a centralized imperial state. The flaw was that while farmers received equal tracts of land, Prince Naka gave the aristocracy larger areas based on rank, office, and service, so they ended up just as privileged as before. Temples and shrines also began to accumulate private estates.

The prince instituted a tax system adopted from China, levying taxes on the harvest and on silk, cotton, cloth, thread, and other products, and introducing military conscription and a corvée tax requiring farmers to work on public building projects.

And finally, he banned the old custom of tomb burial. Instead of the traditional grave mounds like Himiko's,

Buddhist temples and cloisters with white walls, vermilion columns, and sweeping roofs, multistory pagodas, and colorful palaces sprang up across the Asuka plain. Skilled immigrants poured into the city, many from the Baekje kingdom in Korea.

But the relationship with Baekje was doomed, and its end brought about a whole new era.

KOREAN ADVENTURE

In 660, Baekje, Japan's long-time ally, was conquered by the rival Korean kingdom of Silla in alliance with the newly established Chinese Tang dynasty. Baekje loyalists appealed to Japan to help them restore their king.

Empress Saimei immediately assembled a large military and naval expedition and made herself commander in chief. This was Prince Naka's mother, who had reascended the throne. She traveled down to northern Kyushu and set up her capital at Asakura, facing across to Korea.

But just as the last Yamato troops were setting sail for Korea, she fell ill and died. Prince Naka had her remains carried back to Asuka, where she was buried. Dressed in white mourning, he oversaw the expedition from the temporary palace in Asakura.

Without the inspiration of their empress, the Japanese were doomed. At the Battle of Baekgang, Japanese ships took on the formidable forces of Tang China and Silla. Four hundred ships sank and ten thousand Japanese were killed, while the Silla cavalry decimated the Baekje restoration troops. It was the end of Baekje and a disaster for Yamato, which lost its territory on the Korean peninsula and a key ally, and its link to continental technology and culture. It now turned toward

China, which had a central government and a strong Buddhist establishment.

Tang China was the most cosmopolitan country in the world, with a vast empire and trade routes extending all the way to Rome. Traders and envoys from throughout the civilized world rubbed shoulders in Chang'an, the magnificent Tang capital. As this vibrant culture spread eastward, exciting advances were to occur in Japan.

Prince Naka, now thirty-six, succeeded his mother and took the title *tennō*, "emperor." As Emperor Tenji, he presided over an extraordinary cultural flourishing. The introduction of Chinese civilization led to a tremendous explosion of pent-up Japanese energies in every field. In Tenji's literary-minded court, poets composed passionate love poems and paeans to the mountains and seas of Japan. Courtiers enjoyed *gigaku*, masked drama performed to music, staged at the court and in Buddhist temples.

Marvelous frescoes in the late-period Takamatsuzuka and Kitora burial mounds depict elegant court ladies with rosebud mouths and swept-back hair in silk jackets with full sleeves over red-white-and-green-striped skirts and courtiers in lacquered black caps and long-sleeved coats over wide-legged hakama trousers, who would not have been out of place in the Tang Chinese court. There are also star maps and paintings depicting the animals of the four directions—the blue dragon, white tiger, red bird, and black snake-entwined tortoise—following Chinese astrological rules.

It was during this period that the name Yamato—the land of Wa (Wa being the derogatory Chinese term meaning "dwarfs")—was replaced by Nihon, the Land of the Rising Sun.

Emperor Tenji died in 672. In 708, Empress Genmei, Tenji's daughter and Japan's fourth great empress, decided the time had come to establish a fixed capital. She chose a place called Heijō-kyō, a more spacious area with better access to the provinces where the court was now trying to expand its control. And so a radical new period in Japanese history began.

CHAPTER 2

Nara: The Flowering of Buddhism
710–794 CE

The imperial city of fairest Nara
Glows now at the height of beauty
Like brilliant flowers in bloom.

Ono no Oyu, *Manyōshu*, 328

This was a time when travelers from all along the Silk Roads mingled on the streets of Japan's first real city, Nara. The new faith, Buddhism, inspired glorious temples and statues. But the Buddhist establishment became too powerful . . .

THE CITY AT THE END OF THE SILK ROADS

In 708, a huge clatter of building work began on a fertile plain a half day's walk from Asuka. For two years, thousands of press-ganged peasants dug and leveled the soil, laid stones for foundations, cut down trees, sawed, planed, painted, and polished, and little by little a city rose.

Modeled on Tang China's glamorous capital, Chang'an, Heijō-kyō, or Nara, was laid out on a grid plan with a broad boulevard running north–south and another running east–west. Unlike Chang'an, it had no city walls, for the country was at peace.

The focal point—occupying the entire north of the city following the principles of feng shui as to where buildings should be erected to ensure good fortune and harmony—was the palace, a magnificent complex of majestic buildings with green tiled roofs and red-pillared facades in spacious gardens. Inside the palace compound were the two branches of government, the Great Council of State, which governed the realm, and the Office of Deities, masters of rituals to intercede with the *kami*.

At cardinal points around the streets were shrines to the *kami* and Buddhist temples to protect against evil influences. Monks and nuns in the temples were charged with reciting sutras to ensure the good of the country.

But the real excitement was in the Eastern and Western Markets, where merchants from India, China, and Korea sold silks and artifacts they'd brought along the Silk Roads from Greece, India, Persia, and the Byzantine Empire, all the way to Japan at the eastern end. There were so many exquisite fabrics in the bazaars that the government issued edicts laying down what colors people of different social stations were allowed to wear.

Japan in the eighth century was extraordinarily cosmopolitan. East met West in its bustling alleys and streets. Visitors from China, India, and other parts of Asia flocked to the Nara court, while artists studied the Buddhist art of China, which in turn drew influences from India and along the Silk Roads.

Envoys, students, Buddhist monks, and translators sailed off on trade missions to China, continuing overland by animal cart, sedan chair, or on foot to Chang'an, a journey of many months, fraught with danger. Some stayed thirty years or more. They brought back knowledge of China's advanced technology, social system, history, philosophy, arts, architecture, and dress codes and ended up in high government positions.

Nara was Japan's first real city. At its peak, it was home to two hundred thousand people out of a total population of six million, spread across the southern two thirds of Honshu and most of Kyushu. There were sixty provinces, divided into districts and villages, and a network of roads with post stations to supply horses for traveling officials and transporting goods.

Empress Genmei knew all too well that the Yamato were simply one elite family among others. When their fortunes faltered, others would be ready to step in. Establishing a capital to embody the beneficent reign of the Yamato emperors and their all-powerful advisers, the Fujiwara ("Wisteria Arbor") family, was a way of asserting their legitimacy against their rival clan chieftains.

But something else was needed—a history that would root the dynasty firmly in the past.

THE LUSTER OF ANTIQUITY

Twenty-five years before Empress Genmei came to the throne, her uncle, Emperor Tenmu, ordered the histories of the court and of the major clans to be assembled, collated, and committed to memory. This was an extraordinarily rich body of myths, history, poetry, and song that had been passed down for centuries, orally or in writing—tales of the creation, of gods and goddesses, heroes and ancient emperors, together with spells, ceremonies, divination, and rituals. But no written chronicle survived. The histories that Prince Shōtoku had written had been lost to fire and the records of other clans had also somehow disappeared.

The annals explain that Emperor Tenmu summoned a twenty-eight-year-old named Hieda no Are, who had an extraordinary memory. It's thought that Hieda was a woman and a shrine maiden at the court. She was "naturally bright and intelligent [and] could recite upon reading but once and memorize upon hearing but once." Scholars dictated the chronicles to her and she lodged Japan's entire mythology, history, records, and oral traditions in her capacious memory—a feat less extraordinary in the days before writing came into general use, when epics, poems, and all manner of records were routinely passed down orally.

It remained in her memory until Empress Genmei came to the throne. She ordered Hieda to dictate this vast body of knowledge to a scholar, who set it down in writing.

The *Kojiki* (*Records of Ancient Matters*) was written in Chinese characters to represent the sounds of vernacular Old Japanese and completed in 712 in three volumes. It starts with the creation of Japan, with Izanagi dipping his spear in the primeval ooze, and places the Sun Goddess, Amaterasu, the ancestral deity of the Yamato clan, at the head of the pantheon, with lesser deities, ancestors of the other clans, below her. It tells how Amaterasu's grandson Ninigi descended to Earth and how his great-grandson Jimmu became the first emperor and founded the imperial dynasty. It then lays out the imperial family's lineage, tying them to the Sun Goddess in a direct line of descent, thus legitimizing their rule, and tying the other clans' genealogies to theirs. It also records the ceremonies, customs, divination, and magical practices of ancient Japan.

Eight years later, scholars completed a second historical record, the *Nihon Shoki* (*Chronicles of Japan*). While the *Records of Ancient Matters* was for domestic consumption, the *Chronicles of Japan*, written in orthodox classical Chinese, was modeled on the Chinese dynastic histories in which Queen Himiko had featured, and could be displayed with pride to foreign envoys. It showed that the Japanese were equal to the

Chinese and had a history of equal weight. While the *Records* were based entirely on oral tradition handed down within the court, the *Chronicles* used a variety of sources, including Chinese annals.

Like the *Records*, the *Chronicles* begin with the Age of the Gods, leading into a line of divine emperors, beginning with Jimmu in the seventh century BCE, right up to the reign of Empress Jitō, Empress Genmei's sister.

Queen Himiko does not appear in the *Records* or the *Chronicles*. However, there are spectacular tales of Empress Jingū (201–269 CE), close to the dates of Himiko (170–248). Like Himiko, Jingū was a shaman and warrior queen. The *Chronicles* report that after her husband was killed in battle, she led the troops while heavily pregnant with the future Emperor Ōjin and held off giving birth for three years until the war was over, while he directed battle operations from inside her womb. Some Japanese scholars argue that Jingū and Himiko were one and the same and that Himiko was simply the name by which she was known to the Chinese.

These two books contain the entire body of Japanese mythology and history and are essential Shinto texts. However, it was not Shinto but Buddhism that was to color the Nara era with its pageantry and lavish patronage.

THE GREAT BUDDHA

Emperor Shōmu was a devout Buddhist. The early part of his reign was bedeviled by disasters—the trial and execution of an imperial prince on false charges, a smallpox epidemic that wiped out a third of the population, then an uprising in Kyushu. Shōmu raised a vast army to put it down and moved the capital several times to dispel pollution and bad omens.

Then he hit on the solution: to build a colossal bronze statue of the Buddha to placate the Buddha and ensure that he protected the country.

First he sent an elderly priest to the Grand Shrine at Ise, where the Sun Goddess was enshrined, to make sure that she would not be offended. The priest recited sutras for seven days and seven nights, until the oracle declared that, far from being offended, Amaterasu was pleased, as she was herself an incarnation of the Buddha. Thus, a compromise was reached between Shinto and Buddhism, which thereafter happily existed side by side.

It took three years to make the Great Buddha and there were eight attempts at casting it. More than 350,000 conscripted peasants worked on it and 2,600,000 people were forced to contribute taxes of rice, wood, metal, cloth, or labor. It completely drained the country's resources of copper and gold. Shōmu ordered the building of a mammoth temple, Tōdaiji, Great Eastern Monastery, to house it.

In 752, dignitaries from as far afield as Persia gathered for the statue's splendid eye-opening ceremony, along with seven thousand courtiers, ten thousand monks, and four thousand dancers. The venerable Indian sage Bodhisena painted in the pupils of the eyes, symbolically bringing the statue to life. The visitors brought extravagant gifts from along the Silk Roads, from China, India, Central Asia, Greece, and Rome—textiles, cosmetics, scented incense wood, lutes decorated with mother-of-pearl, gold filigree scabbards, and Persian cut-glass bowls, all of which burnished the cultured, cosmopolitan life of the eighth-century court.

Under Shōmu's patronage, the Buddhist church was becoming more and more powerful as the country acquired

The Great Buddha was an awe-inspiring 53 feet (15 m) tall and completely covered in dazzling gold leaf.

the gloss and glitter of Chinese culture. After years in Tang China, two scholars returned. One brought important Confucian texts, along with the art of embroidery, the lyre, and the game of Go. Shōmu made him his adviser on law, warfare, and music. The other brought the five thousand scrolls and commentaries of the Chinese Buddhist canon.

Shōmu envisioned Japan as the magnificent Eastern arm of Buddhism. He poured all his energy and all the country's resources into making it at least as splendid as Tang China. The Great Buddha was the pinnacle of an extraordinary flowering of the arts. He ordered temples and nunneries to be built across the country, one in each province, with Tōdaiji as head temple, for which artists created exquisite statues of the Buddha and of Buddhist deities in bronze, wood, clay, and lacquer.

Buddhism was the official state religion, but it was actually not at all a popular belief. The six sects of Nara Buddhism were the preserve of priests, who spent their time debating obscure points of doctrine.

Certainly Buddhism offered no consolation for ordinary people. For them, life was, frankly, terrible. Farmers paid enormous taxes to fund Shōmu's building projects and endured droughts that caused dreadful famine. They also had to do forced labor. Copper and gold reserves had been drained entirely dry to build the Great Buddha, and the country was pretty much bankrupt.

Out in the countryside, life was unbearable. But at court there was a dazzling renaissance, not in art but in literature.

Long before writing arrived in Japan, around 400 CE, people were composing poetry. The earliest recorded poems date from the fifth century. Not just courtiers but anyone who wanted to be seen as cultured made sure to mark the smallest to the largest events in life with a poem. In 760, a poet and antiquarian assembled more than 4,500 poems. Some had been passed down orally, others written from 600 CE onward. Through these poems we can step inside these people's lives of so many centuries ago. We can glimpse this richly cultured world in which accomplishments such as the ability to write a fine poem were the mark of the man, in which a man would risk death to have his poem published in an imperial anthology and a woman would risk disgrace to take part in a poetry-writing contest.

The *Manyōshū* (*Collection of Ten Thousand Leaves*) is Japan's first anthology of poetry and many say it's the best. There's a freshness to the poetry, written before canons and conventions were established. Many of the writers are courtiers, but there are also poems by provincials, frontier guards, peasants, even beggars. Many poems celebrate nature and the Japanese landscape of mountains and sea. Poets also write passionately of love, sadness, suffering, poverty, and death. There's often a melancholy edge, bewailing the transience of human life and yearning for centuries past.

One poet evokes the suffering of a beggar, sitting outside in the freezing cold, nibbling a lump of salt and drinking sake dregs. Another sees a man lying dead on a mountain pass and imagines the man's wife lovingly weaving the robe that he still wears.

One of Japan's greatest poets ever, Kakinomoto no Hitomaro, writes of war and death, of the rocky seacoast, and the unbearable sadness of leaving his wife when he is posted to the capital.

There are also female poets such as Princess Nukata, who was with Empress Saimei in 661 when she set out to invade Korea. She writes of "waiting for moonrise before boarding our boats. The tide has risen, now let us row out!"

A JAPANESE RASPUTIN

By the time Emperor Shōmu's daughter came to the throne in 749, the country's economy was in ruins, bankrupted by

Shōmu's temple-building projects. Famines and epidemics put an unbearable burden on the peasants. Meanwhile, the Buddhist establishment grew stronger and stronger.

Empress Kōken was as devout as her father and installed many Buddhist priests at court. Encouraged by this imperial sponsorship, the clergy had become politicized and spent their time in intrigue and corruption. Temples paid no taxes, owned huge estates, and exploited the peasants who worked their lands.

It came to a head when the empress fell ill and was cured by a faith-healing monk named Dōkyō. He came from a low-ranking clan and had lived as an ascetic and practiced meditation and sutra-chanting, which he claimed gave him magical powers. He soon ended up in the empress's bed and started handing out political advice.

The Fujiwara, who ruled as regents, hated this upstart. The chancellor, Fujiwara no Nakamaro, furious at having his power undermined, led a rebellion. The empress was an independent and strong-willed woman. She raised an army and captured and executed Nakamaro.

In thanks for this deliverance, she ordered a million stupas, miniature

Empress Kōken had a million tiny pagodas made, between 5 and 8 inches (10–20 cm) tall, each containing a printed prayer.

wooden pagodas, to be made. Rolled up inside each was a prayer printed either from bronze plates or wood blocks. This was one of the first examples of printing in the world, just after it was invented in Tang China and seven hundred years before the Gutenberg press in the West. The empress had the stupas distributed among ten great monasteries.

She now took the reins of power into her own hands and promoted Dōkyō to chancellor, then to Priestly Emperor. He commissioned the building of Buddhist temples, gave them extravagant donations, and banned meat and fish from the empress's table.

Then he went too far. He persuaded the oracle of a venerated shrine in Kyushu to predict that Japan would enjoy perpetual peace if he, Dōkyō, were made emperor. It was extraordinary hubris to challenge the imperial family's sacrosanct claim to the throne.

The empress sent her own envoy to the oracle, which this time declared that no one outside the imperial lineage could take the throne. Dōkyō had the envoy banished and continued to enjoy the empress's patronage. But a year later she died. He was stripped of his titles and banished from Nara, escaping execution only because it was the gravest of sins to kill a priest. No one wanted to risk the vengeance of the dead.

Empress Kōken was one of the most powerful women in Japanese history. After her death, the Fujiwara reasserted their authority and declared that Buddhist priests would no longer interfere in affairs of state. They decreed that henceforth the succession would pass to men, as females were too easily influenced. It was to be another nine hundred years before a woman sat on the throne again. And the capital would have to move away from Nara's meddling priests.

ESCAPING THE POWER OF THE PRIESTS

In 784, the new emperor, Kanmu, ordered the building of a new capital at Nagaoka, near present-day Kyoto, to escape the bad omens and ceremonial defilement accumulated at Nara. The real aim was to drive the Buddhist establishment out of state politics; while the capital moved, the Buddhist temples and their officials stayed put.

Kanmu has gone down in history as Japan's greatest emperor. A man of drive and ambition, he was as far-sighted and strong-willed as his contemporary Charlemagne on the other side of the globe. He was determined to solve the problems besetting his country and to free the throne from the influence of the Buddhist temples or anyone else.

The new imperial court was on a large hill with rivers running to each side, convenient for water transport. Every province sent their tax revenues for the year to Nagaoka together with the materials needed for the construction. Three hundred thousand men worked day and night, with barely enough food and clothing. Just five months after they started, the emperor moved into the new palace.

But the project was jinxed from the start. The court had barely moved in when the Fujiwara official in charge—the principal architect of the new city and the royal favorite—was murdered. Kanmu's brother, Prince Sawara, was blamed, exiled, then strangled. Shortly afterward, Kanmu's twelve-year-old son fell ill, possessed, it was said, by the prince's angry spirit. No matter how many offerings were made or prayers sent up, he did not get better. Then came terrible drought and famine. The streets of the capital were clogged with sick and dying people.

The ghost was hastily promoted posthumously to emperor and the child recovered, but it was obvious that the haunted capital had to be abandoned.

In 793, under cover of a hunting trip, joined by his royal diviners, Kanmu set out to look for a new location for his capital. This time it would be perfect. And so a new era began with the building of a glorious city, which was to be the capital for a thousand years and which we now know as Kyoto.

CHAPTER 3

Heian: City of Purple Hills and Crystal Streams

794–1180

I name this city Heian-kyō—
the Capital of Peace and Tranquility

Emperor Kanmu, 794

In centuries to come, Japanese would look back on the Heian period as a golden age, when courtly culture reached its apogee. Cocooned against misfortune, women whose hair swept the ground perfected the arts of fashion, poetry, incense mixing, and beauty. Some created immortal novels such as *The Tale of Genji*, which was to form the bedrock of Japanese culture forever after. But such an inward-looking society held the seeds of its own destruction . . .

PEACE AND TRANQUILITY

In the tenth month of 794, Emperor Kanmu, elderly by now, trundled by ox-drawn carriage from Nagaoka to his new capital accompanied by a grand procession of lords and ladies, soldiers in ceremonial armor, heralds, guards, baggage carriers, and multitudes of attendants.

Heian-kyō, "the Capital of Peace and Tranquility," was set in a bowl-shaped valley surrounded by tree-clad hills and perfectly fulfilled the requirements of feng shui. To the northeast, the unlucky direction, was Mount Hiei, where a Buddhist community formed a religious bulwark against evil influences. Two rivers linked the city to the sea and roads led out to the eastern provinces. Poets called it the City of Purple Hills and Crystal Streams.

Here vermilion-painted palaces, slender-pillared temples, and spacious mansions of wood with wattled roofs sprang up. Lavishly decorated ox carts with huge wooden wheels rumbled up and down the long, straight streets carrying noblemen and princes, attended by retinues of liveried outriders. Like Nara, the city was laid out like a giant chess board, but on a much grander scale. Canals lined with willow trees rippled down the center of the streets.

Visible from every part of the city were the gleaming, red-lacquered buildings and green-tiled roofs of the imperial palace in the north, surrounded by earthen walls. An army of workers labored night and day to erect the two hundred buildings, towers, and covered walkways. In spring, the gardens, lake, and delicate pavilions were swathed in cherry blossom.

Most magnificent of all was the Great Hall of State, with a roof of emerald-green tiles supported by fifty-two pillars. Right in the center, under a canopy surmounted by golden phoenixes, was the Imperial Throne with two pagodas, the White Tiger Tower and the Blue Dragon Tower, to left and right. Ministers, bureaucrats, and civil servants thronged its halls, along with crowds of courtiers. South of the palace was the Sacred Spring Garden, with ponds and hanging pavilions, where parties, dinners, dancing exhibitions, poetry contests, and other entertainments took place.

From the palace, a broad boulevard swept through the city to the Rashōmon Gate. There were two Buddhist temples, one on each side of the central avenue. The rest were kept well away, outside the city limits. There were shrines to all the important *kami* and two enormous market-places, the East and West Markets, where shoppers stocked up on rice, silk, sake, and everything else they might need.

For the nobles, there were grand estates with landscaped gardens. Lesser folk lived in humbler dwellings, staffing the estates and the government ministries, preparing food, weaving silk, cleaning, and laboring.

Emperor Kanmu (735–806) was Japan's greatest emperor, the Charlemagne of Japan.

Kanmu was not a man to rest on his laurels. His grand ambition was to bring the entire island of Honshu under his sway, including the untamed northeast. The new capital provided access to these remote areas.

HORSEMEN OF THE NORTH

In 789, Kanmu sent an army four thousand strong marching north to the Emishi homeland. This was a conscript army, mainly infantry, weighed down with wooden shields and bows and arrows and dragging heavy catapults. The soldiers had to provide their own food, clothing, and equipment.

The Emishi, who may have been descendants of the displaced Jōmon, were led by their king, Aterui. The Yamato, perhaps attempting to defuse the threat, described them as barbarians who lived in holes, wore furs, and drank blood. In reality, they were formidable horsemen, adept at carrying out dazzling guerrilla attacks, firing volleys of arrows while galloping at full speed, "gathering together like ants but dispersing like birds." Kanmu's predecessors erected a line of forts, like the Great Wall of China, to keep them at bay.

The conscripts were exceedingly reluctant to engage them. That spring, the general sent back dispatches pleading that it was too cold to make a move, then in summer that it was too hot. Exasperated, Kanmu fired off a stern warning. The army hastily launched a surprise attack, burning down houses and crops.

Then the Emishi cavalry, a mere thousand men, came galloping out of the eastern hills, firing volley upon volley of arrows. Kanmu's army ended up in the River Koromo with "25 killed, 245 wounded by arrows and 1,316 thrown into the river and drowned . . . Over 1,200 reached the bank naked," the unfortunate general reported to the emperor, as recorded in the *Shoku Nihongi*, the official history of the period. As for the Yamato, they notched up less than a hundred Emishi heads.

Clearly, unwilling peasants made poor fighters. In 792, Kanmu abolished conscription and ordered each province to assemble a militia of local gentry instead. This new, more professional army studied the Emishi's horseback archery and guerrilla tactics, which later became famous as samurai arts. In 801, forty thousand troops marched north. They subdued the Emishi, though it took another year before they captured King Aterui. Kanmu had him executed outside the capital to protect it from his ghost.

In this way, Kanmu extended the Yamato Empire to the northern tip of Honshu. The government encouraged settlers to move north and cultivate the land, although there was ongoing conflict with the Emishi. Eventually the Emishi would come to regard themselves as Japanese, though the northerners remain distinctive to this day.

Kanmu's ambitious projects—two new capitals and a war on the Emishi—exhausted the imperial treasury. To fund it, the government imposed heavy taxes on the peasants, who also had to carry out forced labor. Many abandoned their farms and became vagrants. Eventually Kanmu was forced to abandon any more costly projects.

One problem was how to hang on to power when the elite clans, especially the Fujiwaras, were determined to wrest it from his hands. Fortunately, most of the powerful old clan leaders had died and their inexperienced successors struggled to find funds to relocate twice, first to Nagaoka, then to Heian-kyō. Kanmu decided to streamline the vast imperial court by downgrading many princes and princesses, reducing them to nobility. He gave them provinces to govern, charged them with keeping the borders safe, and gave them clan names such as Minamoto and Taira. It was a decision that would have fateful consequences a few hundred years down the line, as we shall see.

The Buddhist church, too, badly needed reining in. Kanmu's solution was to encourage prelates to devote their energies to spiritual rather than worldly, let alone political, matters.

BUDDHAHOOD FOR ALL

In 804, a convoy of ships set off on a trade mission to China with two young monks on board.

One, an earnest ascetic named Saichō, had lived as a hermit on Mount Hiei, where he pored over books on a more spiritual form of Buddhism recently developed on Mount T'ien-t'ai in China. He spent eight months in China and, when he got back, formed a new sect with its headquarters on Mount Hiei.

Tendai was a warm and welcoming form of Buddhism with many variations of practice and belief and a pantheon wide enough to encompass any number of Buddhas and bodhisattvas (saints who put off Buddhahood in order to help others attain it), together with the *kami* with whom they were identified. The teaching centered on the Lotus Sutra, said to be the final and most complete revelation of the Buddha's message. Rather than monks focusing on their own salvation, everyone could attain buddhahood. Enlightenment was already here; you just had to see it.

Tendai became the most influential sect at the imperial court and one of the most important schools of Japanese Buddhism. Later in the Heian period, it would spawn popular sects that spread Buddhism to ordinary people throughout Japan. Enryakuji, the temple that Saichō founded on Mount Hiei, mushroomed into a vast complex of more than three thousand buildings and became a national center for Buddhist studies.

During the Nara period, only the aristocracy had been allowed to become priests. The Tendai temples, conversely, recruited peasants for their private armies and became notorious for their rowdy monks.

Saichō also brought back tea seeds from China. Emperor Saga, Kanmu's son, encouraged the cultivation of tea plants and soon the religious class and everyone else was drinking it. Saichō is venerated to this day under the name Dengyō Daishi.

The second monk who went to China, Kūkai, became even more famous and revered. He spent three years learning Sanskrit and receiving the oral transmission of esoteric Buddhist practices akin to Indian Tantra.

The sect he founded, Shingon ("true word, mantra"), centers on belief in the cosmic Buddha, Vairocana—Dainichi Nyorai in Japanese—the aim being to become a Buddha in one's own body. The emphasis on incantations, symbols, rituals, and mandalas gave Shingon wide appeal among the Heian courtiers.

Kūkai became famous as a pioneer, poet, painter, and calligrapher. He is credited with inventing *kana*, an alphabetic script based on simplified Chinese ideograms, which made writing accessible to everyone. He is Japan's most venerated saint, worshipped as Kōbō Daishi.

These dynamic new sects helped to fill the gap left when the court abandoned Nara and its temples. They soon shifted their headquarters to remote mountain regions. While the Nara sects had been part of the state apparatus, the new sects created their own temples, lineages, and eventually armies.

"WISTERIA ARBOR"

Kanmu was the last emperor in Japanese history to wield much power at all. His second son, Emperor Saga, was famous primarily as a poet. He was one of the three greatest calligraphers of his age (another being Kūkai) and was the first emperor to drink tea. For after Kanmu's death, the Fujiwara clan moved swiftly to take power.

The Fujiwaras were the descendants of Nakatomi no Kamatari, who had conspired with Prince Naka to topple the Soga clan. Their Machiavellian technique, which the Soga, too, had employed, was to make all imperial consorts Fujiwara girls, even if that meant an emperor had to marry his own aunt. In those days, noblemen had several wives and concubines, who all kept their own palaces where the husbands dropped in from time to time. Imperial children grew up in the home of their Fujiwara mother and identified as much—or more— with the Fujiwaras as with the imperial family. Their Fujiwara grandfathers, uncles, and fathers-in-law told them what to do.

The other prong of the Fujiwara method was to make sure the emperor abdicated as soon as he had produced an heir, the rationale being that he shouldn't pollute the palace by dying there. He was then steered into holy orders to pursue harmless activities such as poetry or painting. The result was a series of child emperors, with their Fujiwara grandfather, father-in-law, or uncle wielding the real power as regent.

Every now and then, an emperor surfaced whose mother was not a Fujiwara and who tried to break the stranglehold. When Emperor Uda came to the throne in 887, at the unusually late age of twenty-one, he appointed a Fujiwara as great counselor so as to avoid trouble. But he also appointed a non-Fujiwara as privy counselor.

His choice was the famous scholar and calligrapher Sugawara no Michizane, a gentle, serious man who was an expert in Chinese classics and in composing Chinese verse. The emperor wanted to reestablish the principles of good government laid down in the Great Reform back in 645. He delegated Michizane to review court cases and issue edicts confirming peasants' land rights so that powerful nobles and monasteries couldn't snatch their land, and to audit the notoriously corrupt provincial tax collectors.

In 894, he appointed Michizane ambassador to China and asked him to join one of the regular trade missions. By now the Tang dynasty was in decline and China was in upheaval, added to which Japan no longer needed to look to China for guidance and inspiration. Michizane advised him to end the missions. Thus, 250 years of cultural borrowing came to a close, ushering in an age of glorious, purely Japanese culture.

You meddled with the Fujiwaras at your peril. In 897, they persuaded Emperor Uda to abdicate and installed his twelve-year-old son in his place. Four years later, the Fujiwara great counselor falsely accused Michizane of plotting against the emperor. In any other age, Michizane would have lost his head. But this was a non-militaristic time. The Fujiwara maintained power by manipulation, not violence. Enemies were exiled, not executed.

To the Heian aristocrat, the only place to be was at court. To be posted to the backwater of the provinces was the kiss of death, tantamount to banishment. Michizane was posted to Kyushu. Two years later, he died of a broken heart. After his death, there were plagues, storms, and floods, all clearly the work of his unsettled spirit. The audience hall of the imperial palace was struck by lightning and burned down and many officials were killed. He was posthumously restored to his previous post and promoted in rank and eventually became the patron deity of calligraphy, poetry, and all those who suffer injustice.

And so it went on, with child emperors occupying the throne and abdicating as soon as they had produced an heir. The emperor kept busy with religious ceremonies, which soon became his sole role. As the divine descendant of the Sun Goddess, he was accorded all reverence. But actual power lay in the hands of whoever controlled him: in other words, the Fujiwaras.

THE BENIGN DICTATORSHIP OF FUJIWARA NO MICHINAGA

In 1018, a grandee named Fujiwara no Michinaga held a banquet to celebrate his third daughter's becoming the concubine of his grandson, the ten-year-old emperor. He wrote a poem for the occasion, glorying in his power. The assembled nobles sycophantically repeated it again and again, exclaiming what a fine poem it was.

Of Michinaga's thirteen children, all his daughters became consorts of emperors and three were empresses at the same time. All his sons became regents.

As a young man, Michinaga had been determined to claw his way to power. By now his only competition was with members of his own extended family, the ever-growing Fujiwara clan. In 995, to his great good fortune, his two older brothers died, leaving the way clear for him.

There was one serious contender left: his dashing, handsome twenty-one-year-old nephew, Korechika. Korechika's father was regent and his sister was Emperor Ichijō's consort, Empress Teishi. Ichijō loved his empress and completely trusted her brother.

As long as Korechika was in the capital, Michinaga couldn't rest secure. So he set to work to destroy him.

Korechika was secretly visiting a court lady. In 996, he discovered that the priestly retired emperor, Ichijō's predecessor, was also visiting her and, overcome with jealousy, ordered his attendants to fire arrows at him. One pierced the former emperor's sleeve, an unacceptable act of lèse-majesté. It was the opportunity Michinaga had been waiting for. Korechika was demoted to provisional governor-general in Kyushu and banished. Meanwhile, Michinaga rose to the highest position, Minister of the Left.

There was one more obstacle in his path to total power—Empress Teishi, Korechika's sister. In 999, she was pregnant with Ichijō's second child. Michinaga decided to strike the coup de grâce. His eldest daughter, Akiko, was eleven. He advanced her ceremonial entrance to court to take place just before Teishi's baby was due. Akiko swept into her exquisitely accoutred new palace accompanied by forty ladies-in-waiting, her glossy black hair trailing along the ground behind her. There, even the wooden frames of the screens of state, from behind which ladies received visitors, were covered with gold lacquer and mother-of-pearl. It was all so dazzling that the emperor lingered for hours. Akiko was immediately invited to visit the imperial bedchamber.

In April 1000, Michinaga had her installed as Empress Shōshi. It was unprecedented for an emperor to have two empresses at the same time, so Michinaga gave them different titles, taking care to make his daughter, Shōshi, higher in rank than Teishi.

Michinaga now had total power, and after 1008, when his daughter, Empress Shōshi, gave birth to a son, he had even more. The succession was assured. It would go to his grandson.

Michinaga was the personification of Heian man. He loved extravagance, pomp and display, splendid processions, and elaborate court ceremonial, where magnificently accoutred officials moved as if performing a stately dance. He infused the yearly round of ceremonies with all the beauty and elegance that was so essential to Heian life.

In 1016, his principal residence, the fabulously luxurious Tsuchimikado, burned down. Provincial governors, who needed his approval to obtain their next appointment, rushed to contribute to the rebuilding. The great lords also fell over themselves to curry favor, presenting him with furnishings, folding screens, silverware, wind and stringed instruments, and swords. In his later years, Michinaga took steps to consolidate his heritage and ensure his rebirth in the Pure Land, the Buddhist heaven. He commissioned the building of a stupendously lavish temple, Hōjōji. It was the largest and grandest Buddhist temple ever seen, intended to reproduce on earth the beauties and delights of the Pure Land. The foundations of the Golden Hall were rock crystal, the pillars stood on stone elephants, and the doors and roof tiles were of gold and silver. The interior was decorated in gold, silver, lapis lazuli, and jewels. Fittingly for such a monument to vainglory, it burned down in 1053 and was never rebuilt.

When Michinaga was on his deathbed, ten thousand priests were ordered to pray for his recovery. After his death, in 1027, he was eulogized in lengthy volumes with titles such as "Tales of Glory and Splendor" as a man of faultless taste, impeccable manners, excellent breeding, and superior brain. In reality, he does not seem to have been the wisest or greatest of men, nor did he bring about epoch-making changes or instigate great policy reforms. He did not change the course of history or create monuments of which people could say, "Michinaga built that." He was not the greatest of poets either.

What he did have was unquenchable ambition and immense personal power, achieved not through military victories but by shrewd political moves and brilliant strategic marriages, combined with a sizable dash of luck. He ruled over a society in which the worst possible punishment was not execution, as it would become in later, more warlike ages, but banishment. It was a period of extraordinary peace.

Lady Murasaki, a seventeenth-century portrait by Tosa Mitsuoki: Heian court ladies had hair that trailed on the ground and wore many layers of kimonos.

THE WORLD OF THE SHINING PRINCE

One person who didn't share Michinaga's high opinion of himself was Murasaki Shikibu, author of *The Tale of Genji*. She records his obnoxious behavior while drunk and how she lay, not daring to move, when he came knocking on her door at night. In the morning, he sent her a poem to which she brushed a caustic reply.

Under the rule of the Fujiwaras, the country basked in nearly three centuries of peace and prosperity. For the pampered aristocrats of the Heian court, it was a time of unending leisure, which they filled with the pursuit of art, beauty, and love. While the peasants sweated to produce the rice that fed them, they spent their days moon viewing, writing poems, mixing incense, playing elaborate games, and turning love itself into an art form. While men wrote stilted poems in Chinese, women were forbidden to study Chinese and instead learned *kana*, the syllabary invented by Kūkai, in theory so that they could read the Buddhist scriptures. The sophisticated Heian

Tale of Genji *scroll, created around 1120 to 1140, depicting a lady receiving guests from behind a screen*

court ladies, however, found other uses for *kana*. They kept diaries and wrote novels in free-flowing Japanese, recording in lavish detail their lives and what they felt about everything that was going on.

The pinnacle was *The Tale of Genji*, celebrated as the world's first novel. Written around 1006, it's an incredibly sophisticated work that takes us inside that very different yet strangely modern world. Prince Genji, the Shining One, is the ultimate man: handsome, charming, and of course a superlative poet, but also kindhearted. He is human and flawed, a breaker of hearts and fatally prone to falling in love. In the novel, Murasaki recounts his adventures, travels, love affairs, and tragedies.

This was a world in which women lived away from the sight of men, in windowless, unheated houses, shadowy by day, lit with oil lamps and tapers by night. They received visitors sitting behind curtained screens and trundled around the tree-lined boulevards of Heian-kyō in ox-drawn carriages, hidden from view, though they made sure there was an exquisite silk sleeve trailing outside to hint at the beauty within. Men spent much time standing on tiptoe and peeping through lattice fences, trying to catch a glimpse of these elusive creatures, and women peeped through from the other side when a handsome man passed down the street. In this small, becalmed world, beauty and fashion were all-important. Heian women wore silk kimonos, as many as twelve at a time, draped with the layers visible at cuff and throat, orchestrating the colors according to the latest fashion. A court lady was more likely to suffer censure for a lapse of taste in the color of her robes than for having numerous lovers.

Men and women whitened their skin, rouged their cheeks, and painted a spot of bright red in the middle of their lower lip. Women shaved their eyebrows, replacing them with two gray smudges high on the forehead, and dyed their teeth black. To Heian eyes, unpainted teeth looked barbarous. But their most prized asset was their hair, which hung long, loose, and glossy to the floor and swept behind them like a train as they walked. The focus of all the activity was love. Marriage was a purely political affair, arranged by one's parents to create an advantageous alliance between families. Besides a wife, a rich and powerful man had high-ranking concubines and could also carry on casual affairs with other men's wives or concubines, ladies-in-waiting, lower-class women, and women of pleasure. A man who was faithful to one woman was definitely an oddity.

By now poetry writing had become such an essential accomplishment that there was an official government department to deal with poetic affairs, with professional critics to arrange and judge poetry competitions and compile collections. Skill in writing poetry was essential for everything from courtship to showing that one was a person of refinement and culture.

The courting process was ritualized. Having heard that a lady was very beautiful or had beautiful handwriting, the nobleman composed a thirty-one-syllable *waka* poem and brushed it on delicately hued, scented paper. The lady assessed the handwriting and color of the paper, as well as the wit and appropriateness of the poem. She then brushed a reply. The nobleman waited with bated breath to see if her handwriting and poem lived up to expectations.

Eventually he might enter her palace at night, make love to her in the pitch dark without ever having seen her face, and leave at daybreak. The servants studiously ignored the intruder, although they were well aware of who he was, as each man wore a distinctive perfume that he mixed himself.

Such a delicate, flower-like culture was by its very nature bound to be transient.

THE LATTER DAYS OF THE LAW

In the latter days of the Law there will be none to keep the Buddha's commandments. If there should be such, they will be as rare as a tiger in the marketplace.

Saichō

Long before the end of the Heian period, the wondrous city of Heian-kyō had begun to fall into disrepair. Kanmu's glorious imperial palace burned down again and again and eventually the site was abandoned. Tracts of land in the south and west of the capital became wasteland, where thieves and beggars roamed, and the Rashōmon Gate was a tumbledown ruin where people dumped corpses and unwanted babies.

With all the focus on poetry writing, incense mixing, dancing, and drinking, the supposed rulers of the country had forgotten how to ride a horse or wield a sword. By 1000, the government no longer knew how to issue currency, and money gradually disappeared. Rice became the primary unit of exchange.

The Fujiwaras also failed to maintain adequate police forces. Robbers preyed on travelers, making travel outside the city very dangerous. When a courtier had to go on a journey, he did so with fear and trembling.

Even more disturbing were raids by mountain priests. The citizens lived in terror of the warrior monks who would periodically swarm down from mountain monasteries like Saichō's great Enryakuji to burn and loot, intimidating and attacking religious rivals and political enemies and demanding more land and privileges. Armies of monks from rival temples and subsects battled each other on the streets.

According to Japanese Buddhist belief, once a certain period after the Buddha's death had passed, his teachings would lose their power and the world would enter an age of decadence, destruction, and chaos known as Mappō—the latter days of the Law. It was predicted to occur in 1052.

In this new and terrible age, the only hope would be to throw oneself on the mercy of Amida Buddha, the All-Compassionate One. All the faithful needed to do to be reborn in the Pure Land, his Western Paradise, was to recite his name—the *nembutsu*. With Mappō looming terrifyingly close, Amidism grew enormously in popularity.

In 1052, the very year that Mappō was expected to begin, Michinaga's son, Yorimichi, who had succeeded him as regent, converted his country home in Uji into a temple and named it the Byōdō-in. Presiding over the main hall, the Phoenix Hall, is an image of Amida Buddha carved by Jōchō, the greatest-ever Japanese Buddhist sculptor. Seated in meditation, huge

Designed to evoke the Buddhist Heaven, Amida's Western Paradise, the Byōdō-in is one of the few Heian buildings to survive to this day and embodies all the pristine beauty and delicacy of the Heian age.

yet tranquil, Amida looks down with ineffable gentleness and compassion. Here Yorimichi prayed for salvation, while outside, the world plunged deeper and deeper into Mappō.

For beneath the shimmer of Heian culture, there were inbuilt weaknesses that made its downfall inevitable. While the aristocrats enjoyed their lives of glorious leisure, the rest of the country was becoming poorer and poorer.

By now, the great families, and particularly Michinaga's branch of the Fujiwaras, owned nearly all the land in the country. The money that funded the courtiers' pampered lifestyle flowed in from their estates. These estates were private, inheritable, and tax-exempt, and the peasants who worked them were virtually serfs. Because they were not taxed, very little money flowed into government coffers. It all stayed in the courtiers' hands.

To the Heian nobility, the worst fate that could befall you was to live in the provinces. Once you were posted there, it was very difficult to reestablish yourself at court. Many provincial governors simply gave up and stayed put. Over the generations, they established power bases, building up their wealth and extending their lands. Forced to deal on their own with maintaining local order, these families increasingly resorted to arms, and from mid-Heian times came to form a distinct warrior class. They were samurai—men who "served"—and they followed an unwritten code that stressed manly arrogance, fighting prowess, unshakable loyalty to one's lord, and a fierce pride in family lineage. People still paid lip service to the authority of the Heian court, but real power now lay in the provinces.

Two rival families, the Tairas and the Minamotos, became particularly strong. Both were descended from princes who had been sent to police the provinces and keep the borders safe as part of Emperor Kanmu's streamlining of the imperial court. The Heian government took to employing these tough local warriors to put down uprisings because the imperial forces were too feeble.

In 1028, there was an uprising by Taira no Tadatsune. The government called in the Minamotos—the "claws and teeth of the Fujiwaras"—to keep order. Then, in 1051, the Emishi tried to reestablish power over their northern territories. The court appointed Minamoto no Yoriyoshi governor of the northern province of Mutsu and sent him to restore peace, and after nine years of fighting, he defeated them.

By now these military families had become a second aristocracy. It was these unpolished provincials, whom Murasaki and her peers so despised, who were to bring her world down in ruins. It was hardly surprising when, in 1156, they overran the capital and seized power. The delicately featured heads of the last Heian noblemen were skewered on pikes and displayed around the city. Mappō had truly arrived.

Medieval Japan

CHAPTER 4

Kamakura: Rise of the Samurai
1180–1333

The Gion Temple bells toll the impermanence of all
things; the sala flowers beside the Buddha's deathbed bear
testimony to the fact that all who flourish must decline.
The proud do not endure, they vanish like a spring night's
dream. The mighty fall at last like dust before the wind.

Tale of the Heike, compiled around 1371

As the court slipped into decadence, the warrior clans took power. This was an age of warfare and heroism, and of stirring tales of great exploits. It was the beginning of rule by the military, which would continue for seven hundred years. The stern warrior values became preeminent and ordinary folk, powerfully aware of the transience of all things, sought consolation in religion.

THE METEORIC RISE OF THE TAIRAS

In July 1156, fighting tore through the once elegant streets of the City of Peace and Tranquility. Swords clashed in the alleys, arrows darkened the sky, and the streams ran red with blood. The magnificent palace of a retired emperor went up in flames.

It was the first battle since Heian-kyō—now known simply as "the capital city," Kyō-to—had been founded 350 years earlier. The young emperor had died at the age of sixteen and rival branches of the Fujiwara family backed different contenders to succeed him. For years they'd used the two great clans, the Tairas and the Minamotos, to fight their battles for them in the provinces. Now they summoned them to Kyoto.

It was a big mistake. The leader of the Tairas, Kiyomori, was a great warrior, a brilliant strategist, and a proud and arrogant man. His father, a provincial lord from the far west, had been the first member of the samurai class to serve the emperor directly.

The leader of the Minamotos, Yoshitomo, was an equally doughty warrior whose lands were far to the east. In the battle over the succession, the two fought side by side. The fighting was chaotic and Yoshitomo ended up on the opposite side from his father and five brothers. Kiyomori won.

Times had changed. The punishment for being on the losing side was no longer exile but execution. Kiyomori ordered Yoshitomo to have his own father and brothers executed. Yoshitomo, smarting at the outrage, waited for his chance for revenge.

Kiyomori was now all-powerful. Three years later, he went on a pilgrimage. Yoshitomo sent his troops into Kyoto, but after a month of fierce battles he was killed. To make sure that the Minamotos never challenged him again, Kiyomori had most of the men of the family executed. But in a gesture of magnanimity, he decided to spare Yoshitomo's three youngest sons. He banished the eldest, Yoritomo, who was thirteen, to Izu, far away to the east. He also had his eye on Yoshitomo's concubine, whose beauty was legendary. He promised to spare her two infant sons if she would send them to a Buddhist monastery and become his mistress. It was a fateful decision.

He then named himself regent, the first samurai in the country's history to take power. Modeling himself on the

Fujiwaras, he lorded it over the Heian courtiers and installed his relatives in key positions. He even married his daughter to the eleven-year-old emperor. In 1180, the emperor abdicated and Kiyomori's two-year-old grandson succeeded him.

The following winter, just as he'd reached the pinnacle of power, Kiyomori came down with a raging fever. He called for his sons and ordered them not to waste time on prayers or services: "Only make haste to slay Yoritomo and cut off his head and lay it before my tomb. That will be the best offering you can make me either in this world or the next."

For he knew that the Tairas and their grip on power were doomed.

THE MINAMOTOS COME INTO THEIR OWN

By now the Heian courtiers had grown thoroughly fed up with Kiyomori's uppity ways. They called on the Minamotos to throw out the Tairas.

Yoshitomo's eldest son, Yoritomo, was now thirty and a born leader. He had spent much of his exile in the home of a Taira ally named Hōjō Tokimasa. He and Tokimasa's daughter, Masako, fell in love. Her father hastily arranged a marriage for her with someone else. But she was

This famous portrait of Yoritomo (1147–1199) by Fujiwara no Takanobu, painted in 1179, shows him as a shrewd-looking man with a thin moustache and a cool gaze.

Yoshitsune (1159–1189) was a brilliant swordsman even as a boy and, according to legend, defeated the giant Benkei in a David-and-Goliath battle on Gojō Bridge in Kyoto. Benkei became his most loyal follower.

a feisty young woman and, on her wedding day, ran away with Yoritomo. They hid out until Tokimasa agreed to let them marry.

Now Yoritomo made his way to the Minamotos' ancestral lands to the east, to the village of Kamakura near modern-day Tokyo. This was the samurai heartland, rugged frontier country where rival clans battled for control of larger and larger tracts of territory. It was by far the most productive agricultural region in Japan.

Clansmen flocked to join him with pledges of allegiance and Kamakura grew into a thriving town. Yoritomo handed out land rights and official posts, setting up an alternative seat of government.

His half brother Yoshitsune, the youngest son of Yoshitomo's beautiful concubine, heard that Yoritomo was preparing to fight the Tairas and rode east to join him. Yoshitsune has gone down in history as a brilliant, daring, and gallant warrior, whose legendary exploits and tragic end are immortalized in epics and dramas, performed on the Noh and kabuki stages to this day. He was a high-spirited, impetuous, headstrong young man, very popular among his soldiers and at court. Yoritomo made him commander in chief of his armies.

In terror of the forces raging against them, the Tairas fled west to their homeland, taking with them the infant emperor and his mother and grandmother, Kiyomori's daughter and widow, together with the imperial regalia—the sword, mirror, and jewel handed down from the Sun Goddess, which symbolized the emperor's authority. After decades of luxury at the imperial court, they had grown soft. There was famine in the west of the country, though not in Yoritomo's stronghold in the east, and they were soon half-starved.

Yoshitsune and his troops cornered them at Ichi-no-Tani, near modern-day Kobe, on the shores of the Inland Sea. The encounter has become legendary. The Tairas had set up camp on a narrow strip of land between the sea and a hill so precipitous that monkeys dared not descend it. In a spectacular display of verve and military brilliance, Yoshitsune led a reckless cavalry charge, crashing straight down the cliffs, and took the Tairas by surprise. The demoralized survivors fled to Dan-no-ura at the western tip of the Inland Sea.

Yoshitsune pursued them and attacked them there. The Tairas had the child emperor with them, in all his court regalia, to encourage their troops. The two navies fought with bows and arrows, then hand to hand with swords and daggers.

But then the tide turned. The Minamoto archers picked off the Taira rowers and helmsmen, leaving their boats adrift. Many Tairas committed suicide and soon, say the chronicles, the sea was red with their blood.

Kiyomori's widow took the child emperor in her arms and leaped into the sea, followed by many of her women. To this day, on the nearby beach there are crabs with a scowling samurai face on their shells, which people say are the souls of the Tairas.

Blind minstrels twanging their lutes sang of these heroic deeds and tragic ends, and the story of the wars and of Yoshitsune's exploits spread around the country. Early in the fourteenth century, the stories were gathered together, not so much as tales of chivalry but as poignant exemplars of the frailty of human glory, in *The Tale of the Heike* (the Heike being the Tairas), the Japanese equivalent of *The Iliad*.

Yoshitsune had proved himself the greatest hero of the age. He had wiped out the Tairas and given victory to Yoritomo. But if he thought his proud brother would thank him for it, he was much mistaken.

Yoritomo saw enemies everywhere. He had already had most of his family killed to firm up his hold on power. Now he was determined to get rid of Yoshitsune. He accused him of subversion. Yoshitsune sent a letter declaring his eternal allegiance, then went on the run.

Yoritomo sentenced Yoshitsune to death, then set up a whole administrative system to track him down. It was a two-tier system manned by Yoritomo's most trusted vassals, giving him extraordinary powers. There were military governors to run each province and stewards to supervise the great manorial estates that produced the main wealth of the country and to collect taxes from the estates' owners, who had never paid taxes before. The stewards had armed men to back them up, which meant that in every estate where there was a steward, there was a garrison loyal to the Minamotos.

The immediate aim was to capture Yoshitsune. But the long-term effect was to replace the civil governors appointed by the imperial court in Kyoto with military governors answerable only to Yoritomo.

Yoshitsune finally made his way to Hiraizumi, the magnificent capital of the northern land of Mutsu, the only place in the country outside Yoritomo's control. Hiraizumi's temples, walled and roofed with gold from local mines, rivaled Kyoto in splendor. Marco Polo, who was in China a century later, wrote about them in his *Travels*. The city was far more splendid than Kamakura, which was a crude military encampment at this point.

Then the old lord who had given Yoshitsune sanctuary died. His son, eager to placate Yoritomo, sent his army to attack Yoshitsune. Yoshitsune's nine followers resisted bravely, long enough to allow him to carry out an honorable suicide.

The young lord's treachery did not save him. Yoshitsune's arrival in Hiraizumi gave Yoritomo the perfect excuse to send a huge army to incorporate the vast northern territories into his own domains. The treacherous lord's head arrived in Kamakura a few months after Yoshitsune's.

In 1192, the cloistered emperor awarded Yoritomo the title of Sei-i-Tai-shōgun, "barbarian-quelling generalissimo," granting him control over all the military forces in the country.

Yoritomo's power was now absolute. He paid lip service to the status of the emperor but kept well away from Kyoto with its decadent lifestyle. Kamakura, his capital, was an austere place, suitable for a military headquarters. It was a coastal city protected by the sea and surrounded by tree-covered hills broken by seven passes, with a broad avenue leading to a huge shrine dedicated to the War God, Hachiman. Spare, clean-lined houses with big reed-thatched roofs rambled up the foothills.

Yoritomo's system of military governors and stewards formed a whole administrative network. For the first time in history, there was an organized system of government right across the country. He also rationalized taxation. The staple was rice. The whole country depended on it. But the annual yield depended on rainfall and sunshine. Yoritomo tied taxation to the rice yield and ensured that peasants were protected against oppression and extortion by landowners. They were heavily taxed, but they had rights. They could sell their holdings and migrate if they wanted. The result was greater prosperity, spreading literacy among the military and peasant classes. This shogunal form of government that Yoritomo created was to last in one form or another for almost seven hundred years.

During the war, the Tairas had burned down Tōdaiji, the venerable temple in the city of Nara, which housed the Great Buddha. Yoritomo had it rebuilt. The celebrated sculptor Unkei carved muscular life-sized images of Buddhas and guardian deities to express the bold spirit of the now dominant warrior elite.

Then, in 1199, Yoritomo was thrown from his horse—startled, according to legend, by the vengeful ghost of Yoshitsune. His sudden death revealed his one shortcoming: he had failed to provide for a capable successor. He had had almost his entire family killed off and his sons were weak and incompetent. It would not be long before his entire line died out.

THE NUN SHOGUN

In 1221, the retired emperor in Kyoto gathered troops, intending to snatch back power for himself. Yoritomo's widow, Hōjō Masako, summoned the Kamakura warriors and gave a rousing speech through a spokesman from behind her blinds, reminding them of their duties and obligations and of their vow of loyalty to the Minamoto family. She sent an army that easily demolished the emperor's forces and took over the capital, stationing deputies to keep an eye on the imperial court. The retired emperor and his family were executed or exiled.

Masako was a formidable woman. As a child, she rode, hunted, fished, and dined with the men of the family and, after eloping with Yoritomo against her father's wishes, wore a sword and rode into battle. After Yoritomo's death she took holy orders in the traditional way. But that didn't stop her from wielding power from behind the scenes, ensuring that his legacy lived on.

Her eighteen-year-old son, who succeeded Yoritomo, completely lacked his father's drive and brilliance. He, her other son, and her father, all rivals for power, soon met with untimely ends. Masako named a baby great-grandson of Yoritomo's younger sister as shogun, leaving her as the real power, the Nun Shogun. In all, fifteen generations of the Hōjō family controlled the Kamakura shogunate. There was still a shogun but, like the emperor in Kyoto, he had no power.

After the samurai armies rampaging across the land, Yoritomo's victory had brought peace, and law and order had finally been established. Nevertheless, for the lower orders, it felt more than ever as if the Age of Mappō—the Latter Days of the Law—had truly arrived.

AGE OF FAITH

In 1257, a huge earthquake destroyed half of Kamakura. It was followed by years of cold, wet weather that devastated crops and brought about terrible famine and epidemics. People subsisted on grass and roots, and the streets of Kyoto were choked with the dead and dying. Between 1254 and 1260, drought, earthquakes, epidemics, famines, fires, and storms wiped out half the population.

In such times people craved religion. The Buddhism of the Heian period had been a religion of the elite. Noblemen built lavish Amida Halls to ensure their rebirth in Amida's Western Paradise. Even reciting the *nembutsu*, "I take refuge in Amida Buddha," involved a difficult meditation. Meanwhile, armies of militant monks intimidated the residents of Kyoto so ferociously that the emperor dared not leave his palace.

What was needed was a religion for the common person that could be practiced even in the Age of Mappō.

Then a charismatic monk named Hōnen began to preach. His message was simple. Amida had vowed to save everyone who threw themselves on his infinite mercy. You didn't have to understand the profound meaning of the *nembutsu*. All you had to do was repeat it. He placed the lowliest person on an equal footing with the wisest monk.

His message spread like wildfire. Nobles, princes, former samurai, robbers, fortune tellers, outcasts, even women—who had always been excluded—came to hear him speak.

Hōnen called his new sect Jōdo-shū, the Pure Land School. The Buddhist establishment hated him, as did the shogunal court. Eventually, the regent banned the practice of the *nembutsu* and banished Hōnen to the island of Sado, where he spread his teachings to fisherfolk, prostitutes, and peasants.

One of Hōnen's disciples was another monk called Shinran. He simplified the practice even more and was even more radical. No matter what evil you had done or did, he said, all you had to do was say the *nembutsu* just once with complete sincerity and you would be saved. He called his new sect Jōdo

Shinshū, the New Pure Land School. The simplicity of the teachings of both these preachers and the hope they offered attracted millions of followers.

Meanwhile, two monks named Eisai and Dōgen brought Zen to Japan from China. This was a meditative practice that aimed at supreme enlightenment, a state that could not be communicated through words. With its focus on simplicity and austerity, it came to embody the samurai ethos, and its clean aesthetic came to permeate Japanese culture. There were two Zen sects, Rinzai Zen, which was more aesthetic, and Soto Zen, which was more austere and focused on *kōan*, mind-boggling puzzles such as, "What is the sound of one hand clapping?"

Then the fiery preacher Nichiren burst onto the scene. He settled in Kamakura and crowds gathered in the streets and open spaces to hear him preach. Nichiren was a reformer and a prophet. He preached that the Lotus Sutra, which formed the basis of Tendai teaching, represented the highest expression of truth and he made the core of his practice the mantra *Namu myōho renge kyō*, "I take refuge in the Exquisite Law of the Lotus Sutra." He showered sarcasm and insults on all the other sects, denouncing the Jōdo School as the "path to hell" and Zen as "a doctrine of fiends and devils," declaring that Shingon would be "the ruin of the country" and condemning the monks of the Nara monasteries as "traitors." They were all, he declared, sapping the vitality of the country and corrupting the state.

In 1260, he sent a treatise to the Hōjō regent declaring that the disasters afflicting Japan were because people failed to observe the teachings of the Lotus Sutra and threatening uprisings, foreign invasion, and the downfall of the government if they did not follow his path. He warned that the Mongols, who were rampaging across half the world at the time, would invade Japan.

The regent denounced him as a subversive and sentenced him to death, then rescinded the order (when, according to the story, a lightning bolt broke the executioner's sword into three) and had him exiled to Sado Island, where he converted most of the population.

These new sects were in tune with the newly rising classes—lower-ranking warriors, merchants, and farmers. Thus, Buddhism became a popular religion and spread to all corners of the country. This was Japan's Age of Faith.

And Nichiren's predictions were to prove correct.

MONGOLS INVADE

In 1260, Khublai, khan of the Mongols, made himself emperor of China. Eight years later, seventeen-year-old Hōjō Tokimune succeeded his father as regent. Almost immediately, envoys arrived in Kamakura with a letter from "the Emperor of Great Mongolia" to the "King of Japan," demanding that Japan become the khan's tributary or face certain doom.

Tokimune was not intimidated. He chose not to answer. Over the next five years, more dispatches arrived. Tokimune sent them all back with no reply.

By now the Mongol empire stretched from western Asia to Russia, China, and Korea. Mongol soldiers had defeated the Teutonic Knights of Prussia. Japan's great advantage was the sea, which formed a natural barrier. Attacking Japan required preparation and there was time for the Koreans to warn the Japanese. The shogunate hurriedly prepared the west coast for possible invasion.

In November 1274, the same year that Marco Polo arrived in China, 450 Korean ships, carrying fifteen thousand Mongols and their Chinese conscripts and manned by fifteen thousand Korean sailors, landed at Hakata Bay in northern Kyushu.

The Japanese soon discovered that the Mongols did not fight by the rules, at least not according to the laws of chivalry as practiced in Japan. When the samurai stepped forward to declaim their name and lineage before challenging an opponent to single combat, the Mongols mowed them down. Mongol soldiers were trained to fight as a unit, advancing in phalanxes protected by shield walls. They were better armed, with powerful crossbows that fired poisoned arrows and huge catapults that threw iron balls that exploded with a deafening, blinding crash, disorienting the samurai and their horses. It was the first time the Japanese had ever seen gunpowder.

The local Japanese fought bravely, relying on hand-to-hand fighting when they could get close enough through the hail of arrows and firebombs. They held off the Mongols till dusk, then retreated behind their earthworks to await reinforcements that were on their way. The invaders returned to their ships.

That night, a huge storm blew up, drove the fleet out to sea, and sank most of the ships. The survivors fled back to Korea. Of the 30,000-strong invasion force, 13,500 did not return.

Tokimune knew the threat was not over. He ordered the construction of a huge stone rampart to encircle Hakata Bay, and military governors across the country mobilized troops.

The following year, Khublai sent envoys summoning the Japanese ruler to pay him homage in his newly built capital, Dadu, modern-day Beijing. Tokimune was even more determined not to submit. He had six of the envoys executed and displayed their heads in public. Khublai sent another mission. Tokimune had all their heads cut off.

Takezaki Suenaga (1246–1314) commissioned a picture scroll to commemorate his part in the Mongol wars. The picture shows samurai boarding a Mongol ship. Suenaga, with a quiver of three arrows, is on the deck, fighting.

At the end of 1280, the Japanese heard that the Mongols would attack the following spring. The emperor ordered prayers to be said and services performed and sent a personally handwritten letter to the tombs of his ancestors. Messengers galloped to the Ise shrines to petition the Sun Goddess, Amaterasu, to save them.

That June, fifty thousand Mongols and Koreans set sail from Korea, followed by a hundred thousand Chinese from South China in a huge armada of some four thousand ships, the largest sea invasion force ever assembled up to that time. The wall proved an effective defense. The Japanese fought bravely for seven weeks, with boatloads of samurai making raids on the cumbersome Mongol transports. But it was obvious that eventually the samurai would be overwhelmed by the sheer weight of numbers.

Then the skies darkened and a great wind swept the sea where the Mongol fleet lay at anchor. The typhoon was so fierce that it uprooted large trees. It blew for two days, driving the enemy vessels into the narrows, jamming and wrecking them. The Chinese officers fled on the surviving ships, leaving behind 100,000 troops, who were killed or captured by the Japanese. Of the 4,000 ships, only 200 escaped; of the 150,000 men, less than a fifth survived.

At the time, it seemed obvious that this twice-repeated miracle had been a divine wind—*kami-kaze*—inspired by the prayers of the supplicants. The emperor and the monasteries took the credit, rather than the government.

It was a spectacular victory. But the country was exhausted. Agriculture had been neglected and huge amounts of money spent on military preparations, which put a heavy strain on the shogunate finances. The Japanese had to carry on maintaining their defenses till Khublai died in 1294. The whole structure that Yoritomo had created was falling apart. The old frugal simplicity had vanished, the law courts had become vacillating and corrupt. The sheen was gone from the Hōjō regents.

Money was still being spent on the coastal defenses when Hōjō Takatoki succeeded as the fourteenth regent at the age of thirteen in 1316. He took little interest in government and spent his days watching dance performances and dog fights. Meanwhile, banditry and disorder grew and there was growing hatred of the Hōjōs.

Over in Kyoto, Emperor Go-Daigo laid plans to overthrow the Kamakura regime. The Hōjōs got wind of it and sent troops to depose him. They banished him to the remote Oki Islands in the Sea of Japan.

Two years later, he escaped and raised more troops. The Hōjōs sent an army against him, led by their brilliant general, the twenty-six-year-old Ashikaga Takauji. Ashikaga was a Minamoto and unofficially leader of the Minamoto clan. To his eyes, the Hōjōs were impostors who had started out as allies of the Tairas, the deadly enemies of the Minamotos. Realizing that the tide was turning, he defected to the imperial side with his men and attacked the shogunal headquarters in Kyoto.

His fellow general also changed sides and besieged Kamakura. After five days of fighting, the regent, Takatoki, retreated to the Hōjō clan's family temple along with 870 followers. They shut themselves in and set the temple on fire. Takatoki himself retreated up the hill to a cave and committed ritual suicide.

And thus, Nichiren's prophecy was fulfilled and the Kamakura shogunate came to an abrupt and fiery end.

CHAPTER 5

Muromachi: Beauty and Turmoil

1333–1573

Truly a generation passes like the space of a dream . . .
Zeami Motokiyo, *Atsumori*

After the austerity of the Kamakura years, there was an extraordinary flowering of culture, when many of the arts we associate most closely with Japan—tea ceremony, Zen gardens, ink painting, Noh theater—were born. But this was also a time of unprecedented disaster and calamitous warfare.

SAMURAI IN KYOTO

In 1333, Emperor Go-Daigo entered Kyoto in triumph. The imperial family was back in power. The warriors who had battled to put him on the throne flocked to the city expecting reward, but there was none. Meanwhile, courtiers, who had done nothing, were installed in lucrative high positions. The military had run the government for so many years that the nobles had no idea what to do. It was a ludicrous miscalculation.

Go-Daigo was a typical Kyoto aristocrat—handsome, cultured, an excellent poet, but with very little practical sense. His biggest mistake was to make his own son shogun, instead of Ashikaga Takauji, who had established him in power.

By 1336, Takauji had had enough. Changing sides again, he led his troops into Kyoto after a huge battle. Go-Daigo fled to

Mount Yoshino, where he set up a court in exile. The restoration of imperial rule had lasted precisely three years. Takauji set a fifteen-year-old from another branch of the imperial family on the throne and the new emperor named Takauji shogun.

There were now two emperors and two courts, the Northern in Kyoto and the Southern in Yoshino. Whoever held power, the emperor was still the ultimate authority who theoretically authorized the shogun to rule. But which was the true emperor and which the impostor? The result was fifty years of civil war.

Takauji made Kyoto his capital so that he could keep a close eye on at least one emperor and prevent any further rebellions. Until now the military had been based at Kamakura, well away from the temptations of the capital. But now samurai poured in, mingling with nobles in the palaces and salons. Little by little, the aristocrats' cultured ways began to rub off on the rough, provincial warriors while they in turn brought life to the languid decadence of the court.

The military were now the masters. Having acquired power and wealth, they wanted to enjoy the high life and show the snobbish nobles that they weren't country bumpkins. They took with great enthusiasm to the pleasures of the capital: riotous tea parties and tea-tasting competitions, incense-smelling parties, poetry gatherings, communal bathing, and much womanizing, drinking, and gambling.

Takauji was a devout Buddhist, and under his rule, Rinzai Zen, the sect that most embodied the samurai ethos, became almost the state religion. Zen monasteries and temples supported artists and writers, and Zen monks took up residence with nobles who wanted to be known as patrons of learning.

When Emperor Go-Daigo died, Takauji's friend and mentor, the celebrated monk Musō Soseki, had a dream of a dragon rising from the river near the late emperor's villa and advised Takauji to build a temple there to appease Go-Daigo's angry spirit. To raise funds, Takauji commissioned a ship and sent it on a trading mission to China. For years after the Mongol invasions, trade and exchange with China had dwindled almost to nothing. Takauji reinstated it. The Japanese exported copper, sulfur, fans, lacquerware, and weapons—particularly Japanese swords, the finest in the world—which they sold for a goodly profit, humoring the haughty Chinese, who referred to the Japanese trade as "tribute." They brought back copper coins, iron, textiles, embroideries, works of art, books, and herbal medicines. The income paid for the building of Tenryū-ji—Heavenly Dragon Temple.

There, Musō created the first classic Zen garden with seven rugged rocks on the far side of a large pond, like the mountains in a Chinese ink painting. He declared that designing gardens should be a key part of Zen practice and expanded Rinzai Zen to embrace other aesthetic pursuits too. Zen temples became famous for their gardens, brush paintings, and tea houses. Some became salons where literati and artists gathered.

Takauji spent most of his reign trying to control the clans battling on behalf of one or other of the Northern and Southern courts. The Ashikagas, however, were in a much weaker position than the Minamotos or the Hōjōs had been. While the Kamakura regime had controlled the whole country, the Ashikagas did not. By the time they came to power, the military governors had become local lords. They ruled their domains with very little government control and snapped up the lands of weaker neighbors with scant law and order to hold them back.

Takauji's son, too, spent his reign trying to restore order as civil war raged on. It was left to the third shogun, Yoshimitsu, to bring an end to the fighting.

Flower Palace built by Ashikaga Yoshimitsu (1358–1408), painted in the late fourteenth or early fifteenth century

THE GLITTERING COURT OF YOSHIMITSU

In spring 1381, Emperor Goen-yū visited Shogun Yoshimitsu at his newly completed Flower Palace. Both young men were twenty-three. It was the first time an emperor had ever entered a warrior's home. Crowds gathered from far and near to catch a glimpse of the emperor in his palanquin, borne on the shoulders of nobles in brilliantly colored costumes and surrounded by courtiers, as it passed into the palace grounds, where musicians on dragon and heron boats played courtly melodies to welcome him.

The shogun's Flower Palace was "above" the imperial palace, to the north of it, in a district called Muromachi, and the grounds were twice as large, making it amply clear who was the more powerful. At the heart of it was a complex of elegant buildings linked with roofed walkways facing landscaped gardens, with a lake, a fishing pavilion, a music chamber, and many more pavilions and rooms. Streams rippled beneath the walkways, making a musical murmur. The gardens were planted with rare trees and flowers, gifts of the military governors.

The emperor stayed sixteen days and enjoyed music, feasting, stately court dances, and a day of boating. The nobles wore their most lavish and colorful robes, "so fine that it was as if the beauty of spring flowers and autumn leaves had combined." They played *kemari*, a sort of kickball that was a favorite sport of the courtiers, had poetry gatherings, drank sake, and exchanged gifts. The emperor even served the shogun a cup of sake in an extraordinary mark of deference, to which Yoshimitsu responded with a celebratory dance.

Yoshimitsu had been on the throne since he was nine. As a member of the lowly warrior class, he realized it was crucial to cement his status by winning the respect of court society. He made a point of mastering court protocol and was soon promoted to senior nobility.

He ruled like a king, without taking advice from military lords, the emperor, or anyone else. He dealt with the fractious provincial clans, sending an army to defeat the powerful Yamana family. Then he persuaded the Southern emperor to abdicate in favor of the Northern, solving at a stroke the issue of the Northern and Southern courts. He clamped down on the military governors, ordering them to move to Kyoto or Kamakura and live there, effectively as hostages, while their deputies governed their domains on their behalf.

In 1394, he abdicated in favor of his nine-year-old son, leaving Yoshimitsu himself free to run affairs of state without worrying about ceremonial duties and to focus on what he was really interested in—the arts.

On a hill north of Kyoto, he built a magnificent palace complex, the Kitayama Villa. The most exquisite of the thirteen buildings was the Golden Pavilion. Yoshimitsu would greet his guests there as they stepped off boats onto the veranda at the landing stage. The walls and roof of the top two floors were gilded with gold, perfectly reflected in the lily pond. He held musical and poetry soirees on the middle floor, while the top floor housed a statue of Amida Buddha. Set in a landscape of hills and trees, the pavilion was so delicate that it seemed almost to float.

Yoshimitsu was a passionate patron of the arts. In 1382, he founded the official painting academy. He supported sword makers and potters and under his sponsorship the Noh theater blossomed and reached a pinnacle of perfection.

But outside the glamorous residences of the elite, life was unbearable. There were earthquakes, famine, fires, plague, and drought. In Kyoto, mobs rioted, demanding just government. The building of the Golden Pavilion, lavish patronage of the arts and generous contributions to temples and shrines emptied the national purse while the people lived in poverty. What was needed was a strong shogun to bring order. The eighth shogun, Yoshimasa, who took power in 1444, was not the man.

Noh Theater

When Yoshimitsu was seventeen, he saw a popular and innovative actor named Kan'ami Kiyotsugu performing acrobatic dance dramas. He was impressed, and even more so by Kan'ami's twelve-year-old son, Zeami Motokiyo. Like many lords, Yoshimitsu had a weakness for beautiful boys and, against all court protocol, took this low-class child actor as his lover.

For many years, Zeami was at Yoshimitsu's side. He rubbed shoulders with elder statesmen, courtiers, poets, and artists, charming them with his beauty, poise, and graceful dancing; and he studied poetry, the classical literature of China and Japan, Buddhist philosophy, Zen meditation, calligraphy, and aesthetics at the feet of the greatest teachers of the day.

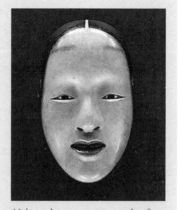

Noh masks are exquisite works of art that seem to change expression as the actor moves. This is a mask of a young woman.

Father and son created plays to appeal to the refined tastes of aristocrats and warriors. The dramas were dignified, ethereal, relating tales from samurai legend, particularly from *The Tale of the Heike*. Performed on the barest of stages to the accompaniment of voice, flute, and drums, by actors moving with slow deliberation, Noh dramas retain their magic to this day.

A JAPANESE NERO

Despite his military ancestry, Yoshimasa had grown up a pampered, effete, pleasure-loving aristocrat. He had no interest in governing and left affairs of state to his wife and advisers.

By now the country was teetering on the brink of chaos. The streets of Kyoto were piled high with corpses. Peasants rose in their thousands to protest against extortionate taxation, unbearable debt, and the visible extravagance of the rich; they stormed Kyoto, looting and burning. The shogunate regularly had to issue a general cancellation of debts.

Yoshimasa was only interested in one thing. He wanted to retire and concentrate on the higher things of life—enjoying the company of literati and artists. He had no son to take over from him, so he persuaded his brother to leave the priesthood and become shogun and appointed the head of the powerful Hosokawa family as his chief counselor.

Then his wife unexpectedly gave birth to a son. She insisted that he become the next shogun. Yoshimasa withdrew his offer to his brother, but the brother appealed to Hosokawa for help. So his wife called on Hosokawa's great enemy, the fiery, ruddy-faced "Red Monk," Yamana Sōzen.

Yamana and Hosokawa both had armies, and in 1467 they took up arms. Lesser warlords joined in on both sides. And so the Ōnin War began, Ōnin being the name of the era when the war started.

On its surface, the war was entirely Yoshimasa's fault. But in reality, the two great warrior clans had been itching to fight it out. Yoshimasa simply provided the excuse.

The two armies entrenched themselves in the center of Kyoto. Groups of samurai fought from house to house, followed by looters and arsonists, destroying nearly all Kyoto's temples and villas in the process. More than half the city went up in flames, including the glorious Flower Palace, but neither side could get the upper hand. The issues became so muddied that those who had started out on the side of Yoshimasa's brother ended up supporting his son and vice versa. Both commanders died in 1474, but the fighting went on and spread to the provinces, where followers of one military governor fought another.

One day, ten years after the war had started, the Yamana side put down their weapons and went home. The following day, the Hosokawa side did the same. They left behind a desert where Kyoto had been and the bodies of thousands of dead.

As shogun, Yoshimasa should have been at the head of his troops, restoring order. But he turned his back and devoted himself to aesthetic pursuits. Having passed the shogunate to his nine-year-old son, he spent the war years planning his retirement villa. He chose a location in Higashiyama in the foothills east of Kyoto and commissioned the celebrated landscape designer Sōami to lay out the grounds.

By the time the villa was complete, Kyoto was a charred wasteland where the emperor lived in a ruined palace. But inside Yoshimasa's retreat, there were a dozen villas and pavilions for audiences, banquets, tea ceremony, incense parties, moon-viewing, and ball games. There was a "sea" of silver sand raked into ripple-like ridges and a sand mountain like a miniature Mount Fuji. Most of the buildings faced east toward the mountains so that Yoshimasa wouldn't have to see the ruined city.

To one side of a large pond was a modest but exquisite pavilion topped with a phoenix. Yoshimasa had planned to cover it in silver leaf to mirror Yoshimitsu's Golden Pavilion, but the shogunal finances no longer ran to such extravagance. Small, delicate, intimate, and low-key, the Silver Pavilion epitomized Higashiyama culture.

Yoshimasa and his circle—poets, actors, court ladies, libertines, and lowly practitioners of tea ceremonies or flower arranging—led a life of elegant leisure, discussing Chinese Sung paintings and porcelain and the merits of poems and calligraphy, admiring the moonlit garden, and composing verse while everything fell into ruins around them.

A contemporary portrait of Yoshimasa shows a gentle, effete-looking man with wide-spaced eyes, a weak mouth, and a skimpy beard. As a military leader, he was beyond hopeless. But as an arbiter of taste, he was extraordinary. After the destruction of the Ōnin War, Kyoto was rebuilt and a new culture, deeply influenced by Zen, emerged, nurtured in Yoshimasa's mountain retreat. Tea ceremony and flower arranging, the Noh theater, ink painting, the creation and appreciation of porcelain and lacquerware, landscape gardening, and the art of linked verse all appeared or came to perfection in this era.

The Ōnin War had brought about a complete splintering of Japanese society. Many people fled Kyoto. The military governors who had been forced to live there returned to their provincial lands, only to find that a multitude of small warlords called daimyos had taken over and broken up these domains, making them into smaller and more manageable parts, which they ruled as autonomous princes beholden to no one, not even the shogunate. They held their own land, ruled their own vassals, maintained their own armies, and enforced their own laws. They fought to take over neighboring lands and increase their territory and the strongest won.

By the end of the war, the shogun had lost the last vestiges of authority. The Kyoto aristocrats ended up moving to the once-despised provinces. Some managed to live off their estates while others ingratiated themselves with the local samurai, teaching poetry or *kemari* kickball to make a living.

Some courtiers, poets, and painters accepted the invitations of provincial warlords, eager to acquire the polish and glitz of Kyoto culture to embellish their newfound power. Poets were particularly popular. They introduced their hosts to literary classics and taught them how to compose *renga*, linked verse.

To write *renga*, one poet composes a three-line stanza of seventeen syllables, then the next adds a stanza of two lines, each seven syllables. Each verse must link with the last to form a chain. *Renga* had been popular as a pastime among Heian courtiers, but it reached its pinnacle in the Higashiyama period. Even a barely literate warlord could compose alternate lines of verse, especially with a sophisticated in-house poet to show him how. Many warlords enjoyed *renga* sessions so much that they offered the poets months or years of hospitality. In this way, the Ōnin War and the years of fighting that followed led to the diffusion of culture to the provinces.

The emperors, meanwhile, lived in ramshackle huts and subsisted on gruel. When one died in 1500, his body lay rotting in a palace storeroom for a month and a half before a donor could be found to provide money for his funeral. His successor ruled for more than twenty years before the shogunate could pay for his coronation. The emperor after him supported himself by selling his calligraphy.

And for nearly a century after the end of the Ōnin War, daimyo continued to battle daimyo, fighting for territory, until a warlord arose strong and determined enough to reunite the country.

Tea Ceremony

In a small tatami-matted room, a kettle steams above a charcoal fire. The room is bare except for a single flower in a vase in the alcove and a scroll with a painting or piece of calligraphy. Your host greets you, puts a couple of scoops of powdered green tea into a bowl, ladles in a little warm water, whisks the tea to a foam, bows, and hands it to you. For a short period of time, you can withdraw from worldly matters and focus on drinking tea and discussing the merits of beautiful objects and experience a moment of meditative calm.

Tea ceremony is at the heart of an aesthetic of simplicity and refined poverty. Every implement—ladle, scoop, whisk, kettle—is a work of art. The tea caddy is often a priceless piece of porcelain kept in a silken pouch. Paradoxically, some of the most valued tea bowls are rough and asymmetrical, as if made by and for peasants.

In the 1300s, there was a craze for gala tea parties. In the 1400s, Yoshimasa's artistic adviser developed the tea ceremony, formalizing and choreographing the procedures. An influential figure was an eccentric Zen priest called Ikkyū, who spent his time in the drinking houses, brothels, and lively tea parties of Sakai, now the port of modern-day Osaka. Sakai was the hub of international trade between China and Japan and the gateway to Kyoto. It was so wealthy that it was granted autonomy and became a free city, run by merchant oligarchs. Here, merchants engaged in the China trade showed off their celadons and other imported treasures.

Ikkyū's disciple Murata Shukō evolved the aesthetic of tea—*wabi*, the beauty of simplicity, poverty, and imperfection, and *sabi*, the luster of age.

Yoshimasa built a tearoom for Shukō near the Silver Pavilion. Dōjin-sai, Japan's oldest tea house, was just big enough for four or five people, with a firebox sunk in the middle of the floor and a freshwater stream behind. Spare, simple, made of natural materials, it set the standard for all future tea houses.

Ink Painting

For two hundred years after 1382, nearly all Japan's great painters studied and taught at Shōkoku-ji Temple, the official painting academy that Shogun Yoshimitsu founded.

Sesshū Tōyō, Japan's most celebrated ink painter, fled Kyoto shortly before the Ōnin War and moved to the prosperous and cultured city of Yamaguchi, on the Inland Sea. Many aristocrats and literati sought refuge there, bringing with them the refinement of the capital. The lord of Yamaguchi took Sesshū on a trading mission to China, where he was able to travel and sketch, seeing with his own eyes the landscapes that other artists copied so assiduously from Chinese paintings.

Sesshū depicts the stillness of nature, the eternal tranquility behind change, suggesting shape and texture, light and distance with great economy. Man is small, almost not there. One of his most celebrated works is *Winter Landscape*, a dramatic landscape evoked with jagged lines and vigorous brush strokes. *Splashed Ink Landscape* looks almost abstract, with smudgy trees suggesting an island and the hint of mountains, but it is actually very precisely conceived, with little houses sketched in near the water's edge.

Winter Landscape *by Sesshū Tōyō (1420–1506), painted around 1470*

Japan Under the Shoguns

CHAPTER 6

Azuchi Momoyama: The Men Who Would be Shogun

1573–1603

Three men are waiting to hear a nightingale's beautiful song.
But the bird is stubbornly silent.
"I'll kill it," says Nobunaga.
"I'll persuade it to sing," says Hideyoshi.
"I'll wait until it sings," says Ieyasu.

Zen parable

This was an era of giants, men who were larger than life. Nobunaga, lord of the Oda clan, Toyotomi Hideyoshi, and Tokugawa Ieyasu were driven by the same burning ambition— to rule a unified Japan after a century of warfare. Sometimes they were rivals, sometimes allies. Nobunaga was imperious, charismatic, and brutal; Hideyoshi able to argue himself out of any situation, no matter how desperate; and Ieyasu wily, calculating, and very, very patient. Between them, they set in place the foundations of modern Japan.

ODA NOBUNAGA, THE FIRST GREAT UNIFIER

In 1560, one of the country's most powerful daimyos, Imagawa Yoshimoto, decided to march on Kyoto and make himself shogun, swallowing up the small province of Owari along the way. Imagawa was one of the last military governors and led the pampered life of an aristocrat. He arrived on the borders of

Owari with an army twenty-five thousand strong and captured two fortresses, then spent the rest of the day celebrating in his magnificent tent, feasting and drinking while rain poured down outside.

The twenty-six-year-old lord of Owari, Oda Nobunaga, had a puny force of just two thousand low-ranking horsemen and foot soldiers. It was hopeless odds. His advisers insisted he retreat to his castle and prepare to sit out the inevitable siege.

Nobunaga ignored them. He danced and sang a few lines from his favorite Noh play, *Atsumori*. Then he leaped onto his horse and led a mad charge straight into Imagawa's encampment. One of his men lopped off Imagawa's head and the vast enemy army, taken utterly by surprise, fled in panic.

Nobunaga had a checkered reputation. As a youth, he was more interested in dancing, brawling, and hanging out with the local lowlifes than behaving as befitted a future daimyo. But he soon showed he was not a man to trifle with.

After demolishing Imagawa's forces, Nobunaga set to work to expand his territory, with each conquest adding to the body of men who served in his army. Eight years later, he was ready to take Kyoto. He installed Ashikaga Yoshiaki as the fifteenth shogun. But everyone knew who really held power.

Yoshiaki, a vain, pampered aristocrat, plotted with Nobunaga's enemies to have him assassinated. Nobunaga had him imprisoned in a distant castle and thus brought the Ashikaga shogunate to a brutal and humiliating end.

Nobunaga was a formidable presence, tall and lean with a sonorous voice. Most were terrified of him, particularly when he was angry. One person who was not was the Jesuit Luís Fróis, a Portuguese missionary who stayed with him for months and had lengthy conversations with him.

Imagined portrait of Oda Nobunaga (1534-1582), unknown provenance

Official portrait of Nobunaga by Kanō Sōshū

Nobunaga now set about firming up his position and taking the necessary steps to bring a century of civil war to an end. One by one, he defeated the great daimyos who dominated central Japan, taking their lands and armies under his control.

At this point, warfare no longer consisted of samurai fighting in single combat but of vast movements of troops. Nobunaga had a corps of loyal samurai, both cavalry and infantry.

He also had armies of lightly trained *ashigaru*, "light feet," peasant soldiers armed with spears or halberds who worked for pay. He was brilliant at logistics, using roads, armored ships, and pontoon bridges to move his men around.

He was quick to take up the latest developments in weaponry. In 1575, he led his forces against the lord of the mountainous region of Kai. Many of his foot soldiers were armed with arquebuses, smooth-bore matchlock muskets, that the Portuguese had introduced to Japan and which the Japanese quickly learned to manufacture. Nobunaga stationed his gunners behind wooden stockades from where they wiped out the attacking cavalry, firing in volleys. It was a devastating victory and the first really effective use of western firearms in battle, which completely transformed warfare in Japan.

Next, he turned his attention to the warrior monks of Mount Hiei, who had been rampaging down from their mountain aerie to terrorize the streets of Kyoto for centuries. His army battled their way up the mountain, killing men, women, and children, and setting all three thousand temples alight, turning what had been a magnificent collection of glorious buildings into a heap of ash.

Even the impoverished emperor wooed the all-powerful Nobunaga. Nobunaga was well aware of the importance of having the imperial seal of approval. He gave lavish gifts to the imperial family and twice levied a special tax in Kyoto for the imperial court. In return, he received the highest court appointments possible for a military man. But as he was not descended from the Minamotos, he could not receive the coveted post of shogun.

In 1579, a magnificent fortress rose at the top of a craggy mountain on the shores of Lake Biwa, standing sentinel over the main approaches to Kyoto. Azuchi Castle rested on mammoth granite blocks. The keep was six stories high with curved and pointed gables and golden carp tossing their tails at the roof ends. Inside were audience halls, private chambers, offices, and a treasury filled with priceless artifacts. The walls, ceilings, sliding doors, and movable screens were all gold, painted with lions, pheasants, phoenixes, and pine trees by the greatest painter in the land. There were gardens, an aviary, a temple, a tea ceremony room, a sumo ring, and a very grand room for receiving the emperor.

Far from being austere and Zen-inspired, it was flamboyant and colorful, flaunting the new style of the new age. It was the first full-blown Japanese castle, an awe-inspiring display of the overwhelming power of the man who built it. Merchants and artisans set up shop and a town grew up around it.

Nobunaga was now master of central Japan, the linchpin of the country. But outlying provinces still resisted his control, particularly the Uesugi to the north and the Mōri to the west.

The campaign against the Mōri had been going on for five years. Nobunaga's right-hand man, Hashiba Hideyoshi, laid siege to a crucial castle and called for reinforcements.

Nobunaga prepared to lead the attack. In early summer 1582, he left Azuchi. He stopped off in Kyoto, staying in his usual quarters at Honnōji Temple. Deep within his own territory, he didn't bother with much protection. He ordered another of his trusted generals, Akechi Mitsuhide, to round up his army and leave for the Mōri lands.

It was a fatal error. Mitsuhide had been the target of Nobunaga's caustic tongue once too often or perhaps saw an irresistible chance to grab power. He turned his troops around and ordered them to open fire on Honnōji.

Nobunaga grabbed his bow and then, as the attackers closed in, his spear. He was hit in the back with an arrow and in the shoulder with a bullet. Ordering his page to torch the temple, he retreated to an inner chamber and committed suicide. Mitsuhide declared himself shogun.

Hideyoshi got the news by swift courier the following day. He made a truce with Mōri without revealing that Nobunaga was dead, then marched day and night to confront Mitsuhide's army. Mitsuhide was ignominiously beaten to death by peasants as he fled the battle. He went down in history as the "thirteen-day shogun." Azuchi Castle went up in flames, torched by Mitsuhide's followers.

Hideyoshi had avenged his lord. He now moved to ensure that Nobunaga's legacy was not lost.

TOYOTOMI HIDEYOSHI, THE MAN WITH THE GOLDEN TONGUE

In 1590, Hideyoshi laid siege to Odawara Castle, home to the Hōjō clan. It was going to be a long haul and he wanted his men to enjoy themselves. He had a town built around the castle walls with tea houses and residences for his generals and ordered them to send for their wives and concubines. There it was a nonstop carnival with feasting, drinking, singing, dancing, and prostitutes plying their trade along with musicians, acrobats, fire eaters, jugglers, sumo wrestlers, and jesters. Merchants from the port city of Sakai kept everyone well supplied with provisions. Meanwhile, inside the walls, the defenders starved.

Hideyoshi did everything with flair. He was a short, ugly fellow with a face like a monkey, but he had an eye for the ladies and was said to have had a hundred concubines. In this society where it was essential to have a long and illustrious pedigree, he rose from nothing. The son of a poor farmer, he joined Nobunaga's army as a foot soldier. Nobunaga soon noticed the irrepressible young man and made him his sandal-bearer, then his stable boy and gardener. By 1575, he had been promoted to daimyo and given a province to rule and was building his first castle.

Nobunaga called him Mr. Monkey or "that bald rat." Of all Nobunaga's retainers, Hideyoshi was the only one who was not afraid of him. In fact, he made him laugh. He could charm people into doing practically anything he wanted. His secret weapon was to treat his enemies with generosity, building up a legacy of good relations, rather than bludgeoning them into submission as Nobunaga had done.

In his grand scheme to unify the country, Hideyoshi's most formidable rival was Tokugawa Ieyasu, who had been Nobunaga's chief ally. The two met in battle but it ended in stalemate and Ieyasu agreed to pledge his allegiance.

In 1585, Hideyoshi accepted the post of Imperial Regent, an unimaginably high rank for a peasant's son. The imperial court gave him the clan name of Toyotomi.

There were two lords left to subdue—the Daté in the north and the Hōjō in Odawara Castle. After the Hōjō surrendered, Hideyoshi offered Ieyasu their expansive territories, including the small castle town of Edo, in exchange for his ancestral fief. The two literally "pissed on the deal." They were now firm allies.

The last remaining lord was Daté Masamune, the fearsome One-Eyed Dragon of Ōshū, who had lost an eye to smallpox. He arrived expecting to have his head cut off. Hideyoshi made him swear allegiance.

Hideyoshi now set about preparing the country for peace. In 1587, he ordered his men to conduct a Sword Hunt, requiring all farmers to hand in their weapons, ensuring there would be no more peasant uprisings and creating a rigid division between samurai, who were entitled to wear swords, and peasants, who were not. It also meant that no more peasants would rise to be lord of the land as Hideyoshi himself had.

Hideyoshi reigned for twelve years after unifying Japan. He loved culture, perhaps because he had grown up in poverty. He studied Noh dancing, became an aficionado of the tea ceremony, and filled Kyoto with beautiful buildings. The Momoyama period has gone down in history as a golden age of the arts.

Hideyoshi's gargantuan castle was in Osaka, the commercial center of the country. There he entertained the emperor and threw parties where he gave away trays piled with gold and silver.

Hideyoshi's Osaka Castle, built in 1586, was far grander and more magnificent than Azuchi Castle.

But peace brought dangers too. There were many samurai with time on their hands, looking for trouble, and daimyos who might take advantage of the lull to reassert themselves. What was needed was a good war to focus their energy.

Ever ambitious, Hideyoshi decided to take up one of Nobunaga's pet projects—to invade Ming China, leaving Japan at peace and moving the battleground overseas.

In 1592, a huge army sailed to Korea and battled its way into Manchuria. Tokugawa Ieyasu, foreseeing disaster, chose not to participate. Thousands of Chinese, Koreans, and Japanese died and Hideyoshi's coffers were severely depleted.

He died in 1598. Hugely relieved, his councillors recalled the troops and abandoned all plans to invade Korea and China.

In Hideyoshi's last years, the question of the succession weighed on his mind. None of his hundred concubines had given him a child. Then in 1593, the alluring Lady Yodo, Nobunaga's niece, had a son, Hideyori.

Hideyoshi was eager to establish a dynasty. Before his death he set up the Council of Five Elders, who swore an oath of loyalty to his five-year-old son. He made his most trusted ally, Tokugawa Ieyasu, head of the council and regent until the boy reached the age of fifteen.

But all Hideyoshi's precautions were to be in vain.

THE PORTUGUESE ARRIVE

In 1543, a Chinese junk blew ashore on an island south of Kyushu. On board were three strange-looking men with big noses, black hair, and spindly legs, wearing voluminous trousers: Portuguese adventurers.

Soon, high-pooped Portuguese merchant ships started to arrive. They brought arquebuses, soap, tobacco, and other goods to trade, while the Japanese sold them swords, lacquerware, silk, and, above all, silver. Within a few years, they were strolling the streets of Kyoto. They also kidnapped Japanese men, women, and children and shipped them as slaves back to Goa, the Indies, and Portugal.

The Portuguese were not there by accident.

In 1493, the year after Columbus discovered America, Pope Alexander VI issued a bull dividing the newly discovered and as yet undiscovered lands between the Spanish and Portuguese empires and authorizing them to colonize, convert, and enslave their peoples. This was fine-tuned in the Treaty of Tordesillas in 1494, which gave most of the Americas to Spain, and the Treaty of Zaragoza in 1529, which gave most of Asia to Portugal. As far as the Portuguese were concerned, Japan belonged to them.

After the traders came the missionaries. In 1549, the Jesuit Francis Xavier, apostolic nuncio to the East, landed at the southern tip of Kyushu and started making converts. Then he walked to Kyoto intending to convert the emperor, thinking that if he could convert him, the rest of the people would follow. But he found a city in ruins and discovered that neither the emperor nor the shogun had any power.

At the time, Japanese pirates were the scourge of the seas. Piracy was a respectable profession. Daimyos with coastal domains organized ships packed with fifty to three hundred men to plunder the coasts of Korea and China.

The Chinese emperor retaliated by embargoing all trade with Japan. Fortunately, the Portuguese were there as intermediaries. The Japanese could acquire much-coveted Chinese silks and porcelain via the Portuguese traders, who profited hugely from Japanese gold and silver. Eager for the Portuguese merchant ships to drop anchor in their harbors, daimyos would convert and order all their subjects to become Christian. If the ships didn't come, they'd order them to become Buddhist again.

Nobunaga wasn't interested in Christianity, but he liked these fiery, learned men. It helped that he hated the Buddhists. In his position, he had to keep aloof from his underlings, but with the Portuguese he could relax. Sometimes they dined with him. He adorned his war helmet with Portuguese fabric and spent much time with the Jesuit Luís Fróis, and even gave him a room in his castle.

The Portuguese sparked a fad. Young men about town dressed in Portuguese clothing, and dishes such as *castella* ("cake from Castile") entered the Japanese repertoire. Tempura, too, originated with the Portuguese, who ate deep-fried fish and vegetables on the quarterly ember days ("tempora") when meat was forbidden.

Portuguese merchants bearing gifts in Nagasaki, depicted on a Nanban screen around 1600

In 1563, a minor daimyo converted to Christianity. With Portuguese help, he established a port with a fine natural harbor on a remote Kyushu peninsula. He called it Nagasaki, and thereafter most Portuguese trade ships landed there. It quickly became a wealthy city. In 1580, he ceded it to the Jesuits, making it a Jesuit colony.

Thus, the Jesuits insinuated themselves into positions of power. Once a daimyo was converted, he became their tool. They manipulated one daimyo against another and could, if so desired, raise an army.

At first, Hideyoshi was prepared to be cordial to them. But he realized that they were converting the most powerful daimyos and military leaders, who might well unite against him. Kyushu was virtually a Catholic island. He also objected to the humiliating trade in Japanese slaves. In 1587, he banished the missionaries and took control of Nagasaki. But he didn't enforce the expulsion order strictly because he didn't want to impede the trade with China.

By now, Spanish Franciscan monks and traders had started arriving in Japan and were quarreling with and intriguing against the Portuguese.

In October 1596, the *San Felipe*, a Spanish galleon laden with bullion, was shipwrecked off the coast of Shikoku. The local daimyo confiscated the cargo and a high official arrived from Osaka to question the newcomers. The pilot unfurled a map showing how vast the Spanish empire was and warned that the missionaries were the advance guard sent to convert the natives before the conquistadores arrived.

By now, Japanese had been to India and Rome and reported back on European ways. It was all too clear that the missionaries were winning over daimyos, who might unite to topple Hideyoshi from power and set up a government subservient to Spain or Portugal.

Outraged, in 1597, Hideyoshi banned Christianity and executed a few foreign and Japanese Christians. It was left to the ever-patient Tokugawa Ieyasu to finish off the job.

TOKUGAWA IEYASU, THE WILY GENIUS

One autumn morning in 1600, two armies met on the windswept plain of Sekigahara, where the highways crossed that linked Kyoto to the Tokugawa lands to the east. There, Tokugawa Ieyasu and his Eastern Armies, with 75,000 men, faced the Western Armies, 120,000 strong, led by Ishida Mitsunari and his fellow daimyos from the council of regents.

The fog was so thick that the Tokugawa advance guard accidentally stumbled into Ishida's army and hastily withdrew. The previous day, there had been driving rain and the ground was sodden. The soldiers sank to their knees in the mud. Then came the thunder of gunfire. Bullets flew, smoke swirled, steel crashed against steel.

Ishida had the advantage of numbers. But in the middle of the battle, one then another of the Western Armies changed sides and started to fire on Ishida's forces. The Western Armies fell apart and the commanders scattered and fled, with tens of thousands of casualties on both sides. Ishida was hunted down and executed.

Tokugawa Ieyasu was fifty-seven and ready to lead Japan. A superb tactician and a brilliant general, he was prepared to use any means to achieve his ends, added to which he was descended from the Minamotos and had the right bloodline to be shogun.

In pictures he looks imperious and regal. He was huge, a mountain of a man, so much so that in later years he had trouble getting onto his horse.

He'd spent his youth as a prisoner of the Imagawa lords, imbibing their cultured lifestyle. Early on he showed enormous brilliance and was put in charge of his first army at the age of seventeen. When Nobunaga came thundering down with two thousand horsemen to attack Imagawa's force of twenty-five thousand, Ieyasu was resting nearby. He took advantage of Imagawa's demise to reclaim his freedom. Thereafter, he was Nobunaga's most solid ally. After Nobunaga's death, he signed a peace treaty with Hideyoshi and pledged allegiance. He then sat back to bide his time.

After Hideyoshi's death, disputes arose among the council of regents. Ieyasu was senior to the other daimyos and had the allegiance of many of the lords of eastern Japan. Hideyoshi's family feared that he was planning to take over Hideyoshi's legacy and rallied behind his chief opponent in the council, Ishida. Foreseeing trouble, Ieyasu sent secret messages to many of the western daimyos, promising them leniency and land if they changed sides, which in the end they did.

So the nightingale finally sang for Ieyasu. He became lord of the country that Hideyoshi had united and established his capital at the small town of Edo. In 1603, Emperor Go-Yōzei proclaimed him shogun, the first to hold the title since the collapse of the Ashikaga shogunate twenty-seven years earlier. Thereupon he summoned all the daimyos and made them swear allegiance to him.

He immediately set about consolidating his position, structuring his administration, and making sure that his descendants would rule Japan and keep it at peace for centuries to come.

There was only one snag. Hideyoshi's son, who was seven by then, was still the official ruler in waiting. He had a superior claim to power and remained a rallying point for Ieyasu's enemies.

CHAPTER 7

Edo: Tokugawa Renaissance
1603–1853

A great peace is at hand. The shogun rules firmly and with justice at Edo. No more shall we have to live by the sword. I have seen that great profit can be made honorably. I shall brew sake and soy sauce and we shall prosper.

Mitsui Sokubei Takatoshi, 1616

The Tokugawas gave Japan 250 years of peace and prosperity and presided over a spectacular renaissance. While Heian literature, fashion, and culture were created by and for the aristocrats and the centuries of war were dominated by the warrior class, the Edo period was the heyday of the down-to-earth merchants. Their dazzling culture of pleasure and leisure spawned many of Japan's most beloved works of literature, art, and theater.

CLOSING THE COUNTRY

In autumn 1614, a hundred thousand warriors hunkered down around Osaka Castle's massive fortifications. Inside were Hideyori and his mother, the still-alluring Lady Yodo, and a force of ninety thousand die-hard loyalists.

When winter set in, the wily Ieyasu, now seventy-one, proposed peace terms. Hideyori could keep his castle, but the Tokugawa forces would fill in the outer moat; for who needed a moat if they were at peace? His men immediately set to work, filling in the moat and tearing down the outer walls. Hideyori protested and the tearing down stopped, but the castle was fatally exposed.

The following spring, as Ieyasu had foreseen, the defenders began to re-excavate the moat, breaching the peace terms. The Tokugawa forces stormed across the half-filled moat and fought their way into the castle. Then a fire started in the kitchens. As the castle went up in flames, Hideyori and Lady Yodo killed themselves.

Ieyasu was now unquestionably lord of all Japan. But there was still one piece of unfinished business—the Portuguese and Spanish, who continued to spread their grip across the country.

He had, however, an unexpected ally.

In 1600, a Dutch ship, the *Liefde*, had blown ashore off eastern Kyushu. The pilot, an Englishman named William Adams, had fought with Francis Drake against the Armada.

As far as Ieyasu knew, the Portuguese and Spanish represented the West, and Catholicism was the Western religion. His Jesuit interpreter, realizing the danger if he discovered the truth, told him that Adams and his men were pirates and should be executed. As Adams recorded, Ieyasu replied that they had not done "his lande any harme nor dammage, [and] therfore [it was] ageinst Reason or Justice to put us to death."

Adams brought Ieyasu up to date on the European wars between Catholics and Protestants and the shogun came to prefer the company of the straight-talking Englishman to the fanatical Jesuits.

In 1605, Ieyasu abdicated and his son became shogun, thereby ensuring the succession. Ieyasu made Adams a samurai and sent a letter to the Dutch East India Company base in Bantam, in Java, inviting them to trade. Two Dutch ships arrived off Nagasaki, and with Adams's help set up a "factory," a trading base.

Japan could now enjoy the benefits of foreign trade without having to put up with foreign priests. The Catholic converts of the troublesome Spanish and Portuguese included many of the western daimyos, Ieyasu's ancient enemies, who would jump at any opportunity to rise against him, particularly with foreign arms and armies to back them.

Ieyasu was well aware of the colonizing activities of the Catholic powers and of the fleet of Spanish galleons anchored in Manila, not far away. He needed urgently to deal with the potential threat to his country. In 1614, he signed the *Christian Expulsion Act*, banning Christianity and expelling all missionaries.

Ieyasu died in 1616, having put pretty much everything in place for the future.

There were still Christians practicing in secret and Portuguese priests hiding out. In 1637, there was a huge uprising of Christians and impoverished peasants, backed by Portuguese missionaries and traders. It was the last straw. The country was closed to Westerners apart from the Dutch trading post at Nagasaki, through which all foreign trade had to pass. Japanese were forbidden to leave on pain of death and the era of the "closed country" began.

AT THE DOOR OF THE BAY

Ieyasu's capital, Edo, "the door of the bay," was an unpromising fishing village on a marshy estuary where three rivers met. But it was well located, dominating the approach to the rugged northeastern provinces. Here, Ieyasu set to work to build a huge castle with fortifications carved from gargantuan blocks of granite and a defensive network of canals and moats spiraling out around it.

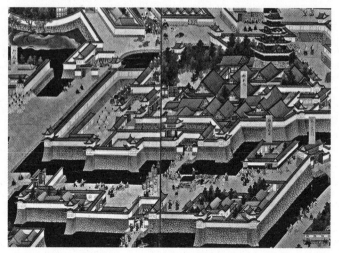

Edo Castle was far larger even than Osaka Castle. Daimyos had to attend court every other year for an entire year, with exceptions depending on how far or near their domains were from Edo.

He designated land on the hills to the north and west for the two-hundred-odd daimyos to build mansions. The "inner lords," who had fought on his side at the battle of Sekigahara, had land close to the castle and participated in government. The powerful "outer lords," who had sworn allegiance only after they were defeated, were from grand old western and southwestern families who had been far senior to Ieyasu before he rose to preeminence and were a perpetual threat. He settled them a safe distance away.

A stretch of flat land facing Edo Bay went to the merchants, artisans, architects, and builders who poured in to work on the enormous program of landfill, waterworks, and construction projects and hopefully make their fortunes. Villas, temples, shrines, tenement houses, shops, and stalls sprang up along with alleys, roads, and a maze of canals that made the city an eastern Venice.

Kyoto was still the official capital and home of the emperor. But under Ieyasu, Edo was to be not only the military and administrative hub of Japan but also its economic and cultural center.

To make sure there were no more rebellions, Ieyasu made the daimyos pay for and provide men to build his magnificent new capital. In return, they were allowed to rule their own provinces with a fair degree of autonomy, but they had to swear allegiance and recognize Ieyasu's position as overall ruler. After his death, they paid for and built his splendiferous mausoleum at Nikko, ensuring they had no time or money left to even think of rebelling.

Every year or two, they had to make the long and arduous journey to Edo to spend up to a year at court before returning to their provincial seat, a system known as "alternate attendance." At any one time, half the daimyos were in Edo, which made it easy to keep an eye on them. Their families lived there permanently, effectively as hostages.

The highways jostled with vast and splendid processions going back and forth, and a very efficient transport network developed with inns, including palatial hostelries for the lords, where travelers hired horses and porters and arranged food and entertainment. At the frontier posts, guards watched out for women sneaking out of Edo and weapons being smuggled in.

There was a strict social hierarchy along Confucian lines. At the top were the samurai, who flaunted two swords and received regular stipends in the form of bales of rice. With no wars to fight, they turned into bureaucrats. The highest-ranking formed the governing class, while at the bottom were thousands of pen pushers, who earned a small salary to supplement their stipend.

After them came peasants who grew the rice. They worked in the fields morning to night and gave up most of their crops in taxes. Then came artisans and craftspeople who made the exquisite artifacts that furnished people's houses, with merchants at the very bottom. In theory, merchants were parasites, the lowest of the low, who produced nothing and dirtied their hands with money. The government recognized the need for them, and mercantile cities such as Sakai, Osaka, and Nagasaki had long been prosperous cultural centers. The daimyos and samurai borrowed huge amounts of money from the merchants to pay for their journeys to and from Edo and for their splendid establishments and lifestyle.

There were also courtesans, prostitutes, traveling players, and outcasts who carried out unsavory jobs such as butchery and executions—so low that they were classified as nonhumans.

For many years, the system was hugely successful. Japan had plentiful resources and a vigorous economy. It didn't need the West for trade or culture. Finally, people could settle down to make a good life for themselves.

But no one could have foreseen the extraordinary consequences.

THE UNSTOPPABLE RISE OF THE MERCHANTS

In the late 1600s, the young heir to the Yodoya fortune, Tatsugoro, squandered his inheritance from lumber, rice, and moneylending in the Osaka pleasure quarters, flaunting a white silk kimono embroidered with his family crest, in brazen contravention of the shogun's edicts banning such ostentation. It was said that the daimyos of western Japan had borrowed a hundred million gold nuggets from him, several billion dollars in today's money. In 1705, the shogun canceled their mammoth debts, arrested and banished Yodoya, and confiscated his property. He was found to have 250 farms and fields, 730 warehouses, and seventeen treasure houses, containing fifty pairs of gold screens, 373 carpets, more than 700 swords, and countless hoards of money and precious stones, among much else.

Daimyos and samurai were paid in rice. Initially they bartered it, but rice was a hopelessly cumbersome form of currency. What was needed was cash. There had been gold, silver, and copper coins in circulation for centuries, which the Portuguese used for foreign trade. Gradually, money replaced rice as the medium of commerce, with brokers exchanging bales of rice for gold pieces and taking commission. As the peasants developed new agricultural techniques—fertilizing, crop rotation, plant breeding—and produced larger crops, the price of rice fell and the daimyos, samurai, and peasants, whose incomes were fixed in units of rice, suffered.

The samurai needed accommodation, furnishings, food, drink, clothing, and luxury goods appropriate to their status. With the country closed to foreign trade, there were no outside sources of supply, so everyone was dependent on local produce. The huge demand for everything meant that prices shot up. Merchants became experts at speculating, profiting no matter which way the market went. They didn't pay taxes because their money was held to be dirty, which made them even richer.

Daimyos and samurai spent their money on luxuries produced by artisans and sold by tradespeople, with the result that, by 1700, nearly all their gold and silver was in the hands of the townsfolk. To maintain their standard of living, they went to moneylenders or bought goods on credit. As their rice salaries generated fewer and fewer coins, they fell into "debt hell." Some declined into genteel poverty. Others gave up their samurai status and took up agriculture or trade; these included Mitsui Sokubei Takatoshi, who became a brewer of sake and soy sauce. Out of this grew the great Mitsui banking empire.

Over the years, peace and leisure and the development of industry and commerce led to a leap in the standard of living. By the end of the seventeenth century, Edo was the largest conurbation in the world, with well over a million people jostling elbows in its streets, and hugely prosperous, with high literacy and numeracy rates.

The merchants now demanded a sophisticated lifestyle appropriate to men of means. They used their money to better themselves. Many *rōnin*—masterless samurai—supported themselves by teaching martial arts, philosophy, calligraphy, Noh chanting, tea ceremony, or poetry composition. Thus, merchants acquired the gloss of the samurai classes.

The shogunate struggled to keep them in their place. As early as 1649, townsfolk were forbidden to wear silk, live in three-story houses, decorate their rooms with gold or silver leaf, or furnish them with gold lacquer fittings—which was precisely what they were doing. It was safest to invest in unobtrusive luxuries—fine foods, expensive furnishings, and tiny, exquisitely carved netsuke, which could be hidden away in a fireproof storehouse. Forbidden to wear expensive clothes, they lavished money on plain kimonos concealing a gorgeous silk lining, setting a trend for understatement as the embodiment of cool. Safest of all was to spend one's money on entertainment and high living.

THE FLOATING WORLD

In 1603, a shrine maiden and courtesan named Izumo no Okuni started to perform exuberant and distinctly unseemly dances on a stage in the dry bed of the River Kamo in Kyoto. People came from far and wide to see her, and after the show audience members lined up to enjoy sexual favors backstage.

Soon, many courtesans and prostitutes were per-forming provocative dances, attracting a huge clientele.

Okuni's comic skits, in which she cross-dressed as a samurai complete with two swords, were particularly popular.

The new artform was dubbed "kabuki," from *katamuki*, "slanted, novel, eccentric."

Men started fighting over the dancers, and in 1628, the shogunate banned women from performing in public. Beautiful youths took over, but men fought over their favors as well. The third shogun liked beautiful young men, but in 1652, after he died, they, too, were banned and only adult men were allowed to perform in kabuki, while women performed for private audiences in salons and houses of pleasure.

Thanks to the Tokugawas' great peace, a brilliant culture of entertainment grew up. Outside the cities were areas dedicated to carnival, where men could forget the harsh world of work, duty, and family, and the rules that the Tokugawas imposed on life. At the foot of the eastern hills in Kyoto was a burgeoning pleasure quarter with brothels, tea houses, and open-air stages. You could watch puppet shows, sumo wrestling, jugglers, exotic animals, acrobats, and jesters, or while away the day in singing and dancing.

There had been pleasure quarters from as far back as 1589, when a stable hand named Hara Saburoemon asked permission to gather Kyoto's prostitutes and courtesans in one place, thereby creating order and generating taxes for the shogunate. Kyoto's quarters were known as the Shimabara. Others grew up—the Shinmachi in Osaka, the Maruyama in Nagasaki. But the most celebrated of all was the Yoshiwara in Edo.

Dusk, when men put down their tools and abacuses for the day, was when the Yoshiwara came alive. You took a pouch of money and boarded a boat to the Dike of Japan, from where you would see the Yoshiwara glittering in the distance. It was called the Nightless City, because the lights never went out.

The shogun's system had created a city of bachelors. More than half the population of Edo were samurai, retainers of the daimyos. Most were unmarried; they could not afford to support a family on their stipends. There were also thousands of merchants and tradesmen who arrived to set up businesses and send money to their wives and children back home.

Women, too, flocked to the metropolis in search of work, and brothel keepers soon opened a pleasure quarter there.

Men visited the quarters in search of far more than pleasure. There were glamorous women, to be sure. But there was also poetry, song, music, and dance of the highest order, feasting, tea ceremony, fun, laughter, and witty conversation—everything that gave meaning and beauty to life. The setting was magnificent. Even if you couldn't afford to go in, you could admire the fashionable restaurants, houses of pleasure, and elegant salons.

A man of limited means could join the crowds strolling the grand boulevard, admiring the women who knelt fanning themselves behind lattices. With a bit of money, he might enjoy a night with one. He might even see one of the great courtesans on foot-high clogs, her face painted white, her lips red, and her hair glittering with ornaments, undulating at the head of a parade of attendants, musicians, and trainee courtesans.

The wealthy man, meanwhile, would be in the courtesan's boudoir attended by musicians, dancers, jesters, and entertainers, all of whom he paid. She would dance, sing, play the incense guessing game, and perform the tea ceremony for him, so that he, a lowly merchant, could imagine himself a nobleman and her a princess.

He'd make several visits to court her, each of which would cost a fortune, and might end up bankrupting himself for nothing. Many men did. That devil-may-care attitude toward money made the experience all the more piquant.

While the samurai preached frugality, the merchants worshipped style, chic, and spending with heroic abandon. Within the pleasure quarters, they could do as they pleased. It had its own ethos, standards, and hierarchy, placing those with wealth and style at the top. It was a never-never land where a man could say and do pretty much anything he liked and start again with a clean slate the next day, a dream of romance with no strings attached.

This alternative reality was called the floating world, *ukiyo*, a Buddhist term referring to the transience of all things. The splendid rooms, spectacular kimonos, music, dance, banter, and genial company were all impermanent. Like everything in a townsman's life, like Yodoya's stupendous wealth, it could all be taken away at the whim of the shogun. The magic of it was its ephemerality.

At its height, the Yoshiwara was home to three thousand prostitutes and courtesans and a huge staff of brothel owners, cooks, maids, porters, jesters, and many others. Most of the women had been sold as children by their impoverished families and trained in singing, dance, and conversation. They had huge debts that they could never pay off, the first being the cost of buying them, and therefore could never leave. Their lives were hard and many died young. But the most successful became celebrities and made their fortunes. Some might even have their debts paid off by a wealthy man who would support them for the rest of their lives.

It wasn't just merchants who enjoyed the pleasure quarters. Well-heeled samurai, daimyos, even the shogun and the emperor sneaked in to enjoy the sparkling company. One emperor was heard humming very unsuitable songs that were popular there, not at all the sort of thing you expected to hear coming out of the august mouth.

We don't have to imagine the floating world. It is described in novels, depicted in woodblock prints, and brought to vivid life on the kabuki and *bunraku* (puppet) stages. For while it may have been transient, the art it created was not.

A HUGE CULTURAL FLOWERING

The great chronicler of the floating world was Ihara Saikaku. In his pages, we step into the bustling streets of Edo-period Japan and meet courtesans and actors, rakes and dandies, skinflint shopkeepers and their unfaithful wives, gossiping shop clerks and offensively rich merchants and their spoiled sons and daughters.

Moronobu (1618–1694) worked mainly in black and white, depicting haughty courtesans in ornately patterned kimonos entwined with their clients.

Saikaku's first novel, *The Life of an Amorous Man*, launched a new genre of literature, the *ukiyo-zōshi*, "books of the floating world." It's the jaunty tale of the irrepressible Yonosuke, who works his way through 3,742 women and a good number of men, told with a healthy dash of satire and humor.

Saikaku's books were huge bestsellers, thanks to the high literacy rate among samurai and even townspeople and farmers, who studied at temple schools. They were printed by woodblocks, which meant they could be turned out in bulk very cheaply.

Saikaku's contemporary, Hishikawa Moronobu, had the brilliant idea of making pictures using woodblocks rather than painting, establishing *ukiyo-e*, "pictures of the floating world," as an artform. His guides to the Yoshiwara prostitutes, illustrating their specialties, were particularly popular.

Nishiki-e, full-color "brocade pictures," appeared in the mid-1700s. Suzuki Harunobu depicted dainty, wistful beauties together with erotic versions, *shunga*, "spring pictures." Tōshūsai Sharaku turned out prints of kabuki actors in strong, vigorous lines, while Kitagawa Utamaro is celebrated for his languid, sensual courtesans.

As the years went by, people became more interested in travel than in celebrities. Nineteenth-century artists produced landscape series, such as Katsushika Hokusai's *Thirty-Six Views of Mount Fuji* and Andō Hiroshige's *The Fifty-Three Stations of the Tōkaidō*. There were female artists too, notably Hokusai's daughter, Katsushika Ōi.

The prints of courtesans were pinup posters. They were as cheap as a bowl of noodles, affordable for people who couldn't dream of actually visiting the pleasure quarters, and sold in vast numbers.

The theater was much more affordable. Everyone discussed the private lives of the actors, the latest plays, the innovations in scenery. Even the ladies of the shogun's court attended until, in 1714, one had an affair with an actor. The pair were banished, the theater in question was closed down, and thereafter the ladies were prohibited from attending, in theory at least.

Where Noh had been all restraint and understatement, kabuki was loud, flashy, full of special effects, with gorgeous settings, revolving stages, and runways leading through the audience where the hero or villain would pause dramatically to strike a pose. Ichikawa Danjuro I held the audience spellbound, playing spectacularly heroic heroes and evil villains, while *onnagata*, male actors of women's roles, played mincing, flirtatious courtesans and were style icons, much imitated by townswomen. The actors embellished and adapted the texts and indulged in lengthy improvisations.

Chikamatsu Monzaemon, tired of actors taking liberties with his text, wrote for *bunraku*, the puppet theater. While kabuki was all spectacle, the puppets, operated by black-clad puppet masters, expressed the most profound emotions.

In 1703, an impoverished shop clerk and a young prostitute fell hopelessly in love and committed suicide together. A month later, Chikamatsu's *The Love Suicides at Sonezaki* opened on the *bunraku* stage. Despite the speed with which it was written, it's a brilliantly accomplished work and deeply moving. Audiences saw themselves in the lower-class townsfolk and recognized the dilemma at the root of Edo-period life, between duty and feeling, what you have to do and what you want to do.

The poet Matsuo Bashō earned his living teaching his poetic art. He was surrounded by disciples, both samurai and merchants, and wandered through Japan, writing poetic diaries as he went. He perfected the seventeen-syllable haiku form, homing in on Zen moments with precision and lightness of touch, as in his most famous haiku:

Old pond
Frog jumps in
Sound of water

Not all samurai were living it up in the pleasure quarters. There were some who took the samurai code of loyalty very seriously indeed.

A PANDORA'S BOX

In 1701, Asano Naganori, the young daimyo of Akō domain, was at Edo Castle rehearsing for a state visit. His instructor, the arrogant Kira Yoshinaka, insulted him and Asano impetuously drew his sword. He barely scratched Kira's face; but unsheathing a weapon at court was a capital offense and he was ordered to commit *seppuku* (ritual suicide). His domain was confiscated and his retainers were made *rōnin*, masterless samurai.

Some took jobs, but others, notably Ōishi Kuranosuke, Asano's chief retainer and a famous warrior, gave themselves up to drink and dissipation.

Two years passed. One snowy morning, forty-seven of the *rōnin* assembled with Ōishi as their leader. They had been playacting to put Kira off guard. They stormed his mansion, cut off his head, carried it through the streets, and placed it before Asano's tomb. Then, fully aware of the consequences of their deed, they turned themselves in.

After a hundred years of peace, such a dramatic display of loyalty was electrifying. To the populace, they were heroes. Nevertheless, they had broken the law and the shogun was forced to condemn them to death. The story was immortalized in a hugely successful play by Chikamatsu Monzaemon. The *rōnin* have been revered ever since.

The shogun who presided over the heyday of the floating world and passed judgment on the *rōnin* was the fifth shogun of the Tokugawa dynasty, Tsunayoshi. He'd been educated as a scholar, not a warrior, and was the first civilian shogun. He promoted scholars and gave lectures on the Confucian classics, established a poetry institute, and commissioned Japan's first astronomical observatory. He famously enacted Laws of Compassion prohibiting cruelty to people or animals, especially dogs, earning him the nickname the "Dog Shogun."

Unlike his predecessors, he was curious about the outside world. The Dutch merchants who lived on the island of Dejima, off Nagasaki, had to make an annual journey to Edo, like daimyos. Tsunayoshi had them appear before him with an interpreter, plied them with questions, particularly about Western medicine, and made them demonstrate Western behavior, song, and dance.

The next shogun to take an interest in the outside world was the eighth. He lifted the ban on Western books so long as they weren't about Christianity, to encourage the import of Western knowledge and technology. Little did he know he'd opened a Pandora's box. Hungry for knowledge, scholars and students flocked to Nagasaki. It was very difficult to decipher Dutch, but scholars worked day and night to compile dictionaries and begin the translation of technical books.

Initially they focused on medicine, military science, and the manufacture of armaments, but soon Dutch books began to flood the market. Every year, a Dutch ship arrived bringing news and the latest books, inventions, and scientific instruments. Scholars began the scientific dissection of corpses and artists experimented with perspective. And so began the schools of Dutch studies.

For ordinary people, life was getting harder. In 1783, Mount Asama, 100 miles (160 km) from Edo, blew its top in an eruption that killed hundreds of people, destroyed crops and animals, and sent up plumes of ash that blocked sunlight over much of the country. For five years, there was almost no harvest. Farmers fled to the cities to look for work, rice prices rocketed, and 1.4 million people died. Rice riots spread across the country.

That year, 1787, the eleventh shogun, Ienari, came to power. His councillors carried out austerity programs, built workhouses for the homeless, and tried to send farmers back to their lands, but it did not occur to them to increase the national wealth by permitting foreign trade.

More than two hundred years after Ieyasu led his men to the fishing village at the door of the bay, the country had changed beyond recognition. It was now a highly sophisticated society with bookshops, libraries, and block-printed handbill newspapers keeping people informed about what was going on. Throngs of people filled the pleasure quarters and salons and traveled the crowded highways, mixing, mingling, and exchanging ideas.

In the schools, students met teachers with new ideas and discussed the state of the country. Some advocated a return to the old traditions, like the worship of the gods and respect for the emperor. Others pondered whether the answer was to restore the emperor to a political as well as a ceremonial role.

Scholars of Dutch studies had a particularly acute awareness of the world outside. There were increasing incursions of foreigners, especially Russian explorers and traders, into islands north of Japan such as Ezo (now Hokkaido), then home to the Ainu people. In 1787, Hayashi Shihei wrote criticizing the shogunate for its ignorance of the world and advocating the need for a strong navy. He was placed under house arrest for having discussed national defense without official sanction. Twenty-five years later, the shogunate, belatedly responding to his concerns, opened an office for the translation of foreign books—not just Dutch but English and Russian, and particularly books on military science and technology.

Then in 1839, the First Opium War broke out, with British warships bombarding Canton. The Japanese saw with dismay how China crumbled before Western weaponry.

The Tokugawas' two great enemies, the powerful southwestern clans of Satsuma and Chōshū, were still waiting for revenge after their defeat at Sekigahara. At first cock crow every new year, the elders of Chōshū asked the daimyo the formulaic question: "Has the time come to begin the subjugation of the shogunate?"

And every year, he answered, "It is still too early; the time has not yet come."

But it was getting closer.

Geisha

In 1750, a woman named Kikuya appeared, not in the fancy, overpriced Yoshiwara, but in the far cooler district of Fukagawa. She played the banjo-like shamisen and sang and decided to make entertaining, not prostitution, her profession. She called herself a *gei-sha*—"arts person." The word had been used for the jesters and drum bearers who entertained customers waiting to see the courtesans. She was the first woman to take the title.

Originally the courtesans were famed for their singing and dancing skills, but over time they had become too grand to play music or dance. From the end of the 1600s, the women of the pleasure quarters began to specialize. Some were entertainers and others sold sex.

The geisha were more modest than the overblown courtesans. While the courtesans tied their obis (sashes) at the front in a huge knot, suggesting that if a man was lucky he might have the chance to untie it, the geisha wore theirs modestly tied at the back. They dressed less flamboyantly and wore their hair in a simple knot rather than the courtesans' pompadours studded with hairpins. Geisha were famous for their repartee and above all for their *iki*, chic.

There were geisha in the pleasure quarters, but the town geisha were not bound by the same restrictions. Little by little, it became more fashionable to have a chic geisha on your arm than a painted courtesan. Having the means to support a beautiful geisha showed a man's wealth and power.

The epitome of chic was the Fukagawa geisha wearing clogs with no socks on a snowy day.

CHAPTER 8

Bakumatsu: Fall of the Tokugawa
1853–1868

*The advent of foreigners rang the knell of the Shogun's
power and of the feudal system.*

Algernon Mitford, *Feudalism in Japan*, November 1911

The arrival of Westerners barging in on Japan's long isolation
ignited smoldering unrest. The southwestern clans of Satsuma
and Chōshū took the lead in bringing about regime change.
The Western powers, particularly the British, played a pivotal
role in deciding what form Japan would take at the end of it.
And thus the Meiji Restoration—which should be called a
revolution—took place.

THE COMING OF THE BARBARIANS

One fateful day in July 1853, fishermen casting their nets at the
mouth of Edo Bay saw four monstrous ships steaming toward
them, belching smoke. They were larger than any ships they'd
ever seen and moving with what seemed like inhuman speed.
The foreign invaders had arrived. That night, a comet flashed
across the sky like a harbinger of doom.

In Edo, there was panic. The government declared a state of
emergency. People stocked up on food, weapons, and armor,
or grabbed their possessions and fled the city.

Commodore Matthew C. Perry, the commander of the
Black Ships, as the Japanese called them, carried letters from

To Japanese, the "Black Ships" looked monstrous and they had far more fire power than the Japanese could possibly muster.

the American president, Millard Fillmore, demanding access to Japanese ports for American whaling ships and humane treatment for American castaways. Perry, "Old Bruin," a gruff and arrogant character, insisted on speaking only to the highest-ranking man in the land. After a week, he emerged from his cabin and stepped ashore. Flanked by two huge black stewards and accompanied by a band blaring out "Hail, Columbia," he presented his letters. He would return the following year for an answer, he declared ominously, and with a much larger fleet.

Perry's arrival plunged the shogunate into crisis. To keep him at bay, they needed the daimyos, each of whom had his own army, to contribute troops. But this meant they had to canvas their opinion on what to do if Perry returned. Up to now, they had always commanded the daimyos; the very word "shogun" meant "barbarian-quelling generalissimo." They had certainly never stooped to consult the hostile southwestern lords.

Shimazu Nariakira, the wise daimyo of the powerful southwestern domain of Satsuma, and the brilliant young

Tokugawa Yoshinobu, then known as Hitotsubashi Keiki, argued that Japan needed urgently to reform, to open up to overseas trade and acquire Western technology. Yoshinobu was related to the shogun and in the line of succession. Nariakira and other enlightened daimyos were convinced that at this time of crisis he was the man best able to lead the country and wanted to ensure he succeeded the weakminded thirteenth shogun, Iesada, but there were many hardline daimyos who wanted nothing to do with the West and who opposed him.

Perry returned the following year and forced the Japanese to sign the Treaty of Kanagawa, opening two ports to American ships. A secret extra clause provided for an American consul to come and live in Japan.

Two years later, to Japanese dismay, an American consul duly arrived. Townsend Harris was a stern, failed businessman who would not take "no" for an answer; his brief was to negotiate a commercial treaty. He settled in the port of Shimoda and after sixteen months of wrangling was allowed to enter Edo, the first non-Dutch Westerner to do so. Perry's threat had been his fearsome cannons. Harris's was the formidable British navy, at that moment wreaking havoc on China in the Second Opium War. The Harris Treaty opened seven ports to American ships, allowed Americans to settle, trade, and set tariff rates in their own favor and, worst of all from the Japanese viewpoint, exempted Americans from Japanese law.

The shogunate had agreed to the treaty under duress. Before they signed, they had to get the consent of the newly empowered daimyos, many of whom hated having foreigners on Japanese soil. To sign the treaty might spark civil war. But if they didn't, the British might overrun Japan.

The senior councillor Hotta Masayoshi came up with a solution. The emperor was universally revered as the direct descendant of the Sun Goddess. If he approved the treaty, that would neutralize the daimyos' opposition.

Hotta assumed that the twenty-seven-year-old Emperor Kōmei would automatically give his assent. The emperors were effectively dependents of the shogun, living on a meager allowance in their Kyoto palace. But Kōmei refused. He wanted the barbarians expelled. Hotta's ploy had moved the emperor from the sidelines into the center of the fray.

The shogunate hastily installed a new leader, Ii Naosuke, with the status of regent: effectively dictator. He signed the treaty in defiance of the emperor's wishes, branding the shogunate disrespectful of the emperor and further weakening its position.

Twelve days later, the British high commissioner, Lord Elgin, sailed in from China. The Japanese buckled and signed identical treaties with the British, the Dutch, the French, and the Russians.

Then the weak-minded shogun, Iesada, died under suspicious circumstances. Instead of the highly capable Yoshinobu, Ii installed a child who would not threaten his own power. He purged his opponents, executing some and putting Yoshinobu and other reformist leaders under house arrest.

All this sparked an explosion of anger that spread through the samurai class.

"HONOR THE EMPEROR AND EXPEL THE BARBARIANS!"

One cold March morning in 1860, eighteen samurai disguised as farmers in straw raincoats were lurking on the narrow bridge leading to the Sakuradamon Gate of Edo Castle. As Ii's palanquin passed by, they leapt forward, shot him with a Colt pistol copied from one Perry had given the shogunate, and lopped off his head.

The insurgents were inspired by Yoshida Shōin, a brilliant young Chōshū scholar and activist who had stowed away on Perry's flagship, demanding to be taken to the United States to learn Western science. The Americans handed him back to the shogunate, who sent him to the Chōshū capital Hagi under house arrest. He urged "men of high purpose," *shishi*, driven by passionate loyalty to the emperor, to rise up and lead the people to unite the country.

These rebels rejected the norms of Tokugawa society. They dressed scruffily, wore their hair in ponytails, and hid out in the geisha quarters or in the Chōshū compound in Kyoto where the shogun's police were barred. They drank hard, argued late into the night, and called each other *dōshi*, "comrade."

Some had been sent by their daimyos—mainly the southwestern lords—to swordsmanship and gunnery schools in Edo to prepare to resist the foreigners. Others had left their domains of their own accord and become *rōnin*. They demanded that the shogunate hand back power to the emperor. Their rallying cry was *sonnō jōi*, "Honor the emperor and expel the barbarians!"

Many gravitated to the emperor's city, Kyoto, where nobles of the imperial court, resentful of playing second fiddle to the shogunate, supported and protected them. There they launched a "festival of blood," terrorizing Kyoto with a spate of assassinations they called "heavenly punishment." A court official suspected of spying for the shogunate was murdered in his bath and his head stuck on a pole near the riverbank with a placard giving the reason for his death.

In the past, uprisings had been brutally suppressed, but at this time of ferment, the shogunate was wary of angering the domain lords if they used force against their men.

Meanwhile, Westerners—merchants, fortune-seekers, and brawling sailors, mainly British—were pouring in. They settled in the port town of Yokohama, which the Japanese had built to house them a safe distance from Edo. Having arrived uninvited, they strutted around, made demands, and issued threats, taking advantage of Japanese currency markets to fleece the Japanese. Gangs of samurai lurked in the alleys around Edo Castle, in Kyoto, and in Yokohama's international quarters. It was a tinderbox.

In 1862, a British merchant named Charles Richardson was visiting from Shanghai. He and three friends had been warned to avoid the Tōkaidō highway that ran between Edo and Kyoto because Shimazu Hisamitsu, the proud and powerful regent of Satsuma, would be passing through.

They ignored the warning. At Namamugi village, they came face to face with Hisamitsu's procession, an army of samurai completely filling the road. Commoners were required to kneel and bow.

Richardson refused to dismount. His horse, frightened by the commotion, rushed toward Hisamitsu's palanquin and Hisamitsu's bodyguards cut Richardson down.

The British were outraged. After consulting the government in London, they demanded an indemnity of one hundred thousand pounds, a third of the Japanese government's total revenues for the year, and threatened to flatten Edo if payment was not made. They also demanded that Satsuma execute the perpetrators and pay twenty-five thousand pounds in compensation. The best solution, some argued, might be colonization.

The shogunate paid up, but Satsuma refused. So seven Royal Navy warships steamed down to Hisamitsu's capital, Kagoshima. There was an exchange of fire, some deaths on both sides, and much of the city went up in flames. The British squadron suffered considerable damage and both sides claimed victory. Satsuma now realized the extent of British military power, while the British were dumbfounded that the supposedly primitive Satsuma were "splendid artillerists," military might being the mark of civilization in British eyes.

In the end, the shogunate paid Satsuma's indemnity. Every time one of the domains offended the Westerners, it was the shogunate that had to pay up. The British began to notice the impact their actions were having: damaging the shogunate and strengthening its enemies.

The insurgents continued their attempts to drive out the barbarians. They attacked the British legation in Edo, then torched the new legation building while it was under construction.

Yoshida Shōin had tried and failed to go abroad. In 1863, five of his followers, with the covert assistance of the British merchant company Jardine Matheson, smuggled themselves aboard a British steamship and sailed to England, where they enrolled at University College London.

That same year, Emperor Kōmei issued an Order to Expel the Barbarians with a deadline of June 25. Western ships had been sailing through the Shimonoseki Straits, trespassing on Chōshū territory. When the deadline arrived, Chōshū fired on the ships and closed the Straits.

In London, one of the students, Itō Hirobumi, read in *The Times* that England, France, the United States, and Holland were sending a fleet to attack Chōshū. He was one of the young insurgents who had torched the British legation. But now he had seen enough of Western technology to know that his domain had no chance. In April 1864, he rushed back to warn the Chōshū daimyo, but it was too late. Seventeen ships bombarded the Chōshū batteries and seized their cannons, forcing them to open the Straits. Thus, Chōshū, too. were forced to recognize the unassailable might of the British.

The American minister to Japan, negotiating on behalf of the foreign powers, used this confrontation to extract yet another huge indemnity, three million US dollars this time, from the shogunate. The powers had realized that there were two centers of authority in Japan—the shogun and the emperor.

By now it was all too clear that terror attacks didn't work. It was impossible to throw the foreigners out. The rebels began to change their focus from what should be done to who should wield authority in this irrevocably changed world. The street fighters would have to be replaced by recognized leaders. The southwestern domains were beginning to realize that the intrusion of foreigners could be an enormous opportunity. They had always hated the Tokugawas. It seemed that the moment might finally have come to overthrow them.

New leaders arose in both Satsuma and Chōshū. Sakamoto Ryōma, a swashbuckling swordsman from the "outer" domain of Tosa, became Satsuma's secret emissary to Chōshū and arranged for Kido Kōin of Chōshū, who had been a swash-buckling insurgent himself, to meet Saigō Takamori, the bull-like Satsuma leader, in Kyoto. There they made a secret alli-ance. It was a formidable pairing of the two most powerful southwestern domains. Harry Parkes, the British minister, gave them his covert support.

REGIME CHANGE

One winter evening in January 1868, two armies faced each other at Toba Fushimi, south of Kyoto. On one side were the shogun's troops, on the other the rebels—primarily the Satsuma clan. The fighting was fierce and at first the Satsuma were forced to give ground.

Then, on the third day, something extraordinary happened. The Satsuma unfurled red and gold brocade banners, which fluttered majestically above the battlefield. The soldiers gaped. No one had seen the imperial banners before; there had been no wars for centuries and even when there had been, the emperor had never been involved. Then they realized. The banners turned everything on its head. The shogunate had been the legitimate government and the southwesterners had been rebels. Now the Satsuma were the emperor's men and the shogunate's troops were traitors. The Satsuma broke into a cheer.

The last thing the shogun wanted was to be branded a traitor. He abandoned Osaka Castle, where he had been directing the battle, and sailed back to Edo.

The brocade banners were fake, hastily stitched by the geisha mistress of Ōkubo Toshimichi, one of the Satsuma leaders. But the authorization they gave was legitimate. The court backed the Satsuma. The court noble Iwakura Tomomi, representing the teenage emperor, had acknowledged them as the imperial troops and declared the shogun an enemy of the court. It was a moment that changed the course of history.

The turning point was when the Satsuma and Chōshū made their secret alliance in March 1866. That August, the young shogun died suspiciously and Tokugawa Yoshinobu finally became the fifteenth shogun. Six months later, Emperor Kōmei died of smallpox, almost certainly murder. His fourteen-year-old son Mutsuhito, posthumously known as Meiji, became emperor.

Now he was finally shogun, Yoshinobu set to work to institute a program of reforms. Brilliant and progressive, he wanted to open to the West, end the system of domains, and bring in a Western form of government. Had he become shogun earlier, he might have changed the course of events.

Tokugawa Yoshinobu, the last shogun, in Osaka in 1867

He requested arms, military technology, and advisers from the Second French Empire under Napoleon III. In January 1867, French advisers arrived to train the shogunal troops.

Meanwhile, Thomas Glover, a Scottish merchant who lived in Nagasaki and had sent the students to London, secretly procured modern weapons and ships for Satsuma and Chōshū. It was a playing-out of French–British rivalry, as was happening all over the globe at the time.

Everyday life was beginning to break down. People danced madly along the roads, singing *Ee ja nai ka?* ("What the hell! What difference does it make?") amid tales of amulets falling from the sky.

Finally, Yoshinobu decided to cede nominal power to the teenage emperor, to avoid civil war and bloodshed when Japan was under threat from the Western imperialist powers. As the largest landowner in the country, he assumed that he would head the ruling council of daimyos that would take over.

But Satsuma and Chōshū were not content with this and neither were the British. The young British diplomat Ernest Satow urged the Satsuma leader Saigō Takamori not to miss the opportunity for a coup d'état.

A huge Satsuma army marched into Kyoto and took over the imperial palace, then issued a decree stripping Yoshinobu of his power. The result was full-scale civil war, ending with the raising of the imperial banners and Yoshinobu's retreat to Edo.

Emperor Mutsuhito in 1872 in full court dress, photographed by Uchida Kuichi in an albumen silver print

There were fears of a bloodbath. Edo was the shogun's city and the people of Edo were his loyal supporters. Then in March, Saigō and Katsu Kaishū, representing the shogunate, negotiated the handover of Edo Castle.

The imperial troops advanced on Edo. Troops loyal to the shogun fought desperately to hold them back but were defeated. Finally, Edo Castle was handed over to the southwestern lords, who began to form a new government.

But the war was not over.

TO THE BITTER END

In October 1868, the imperial army was at the walls of Aizu Castle when a platoon of warriors armed with long-handled swords (*naginata*) charged toward them. The attackers were women. They had cut their long hair and formed a brigade to defend their domain. The imperial troops were dumbfounded, and the cry went up to hold fire. The women hurtled into the troops, lunging and slashing. Their leader, Nakano Takeko, killed five or six men before she was shot. Her sister cut off her head to keep the imperial troops from taking it as a trophy.

After the fall of the shogunate, the resistance coalesced in the northeast of the country, where the daimyo of Aizu was the shogun's most loyal supporter. Tokugawa loyalists congregated there and formed the Northern Alliance. The new rulers were determined to eliminate the last of the opposition and sent their troops marching north.

For over a month, the imperial troops bombarded the castle. Women joined their menfolk in the defense, but eventually Aizu Castle fell. The domain was dismantled and the survivors were imprisoned in Edo or exiled to the far north of the country. Some escaped and rode north to join the continuing Tokugawa resistance on the island of Ezo (now Hokkaido).

Fifteen naval cadets, led by Enomoto Takeaki, had spent four years living in Holland and had commissioned a state-of-the-art ship, the *Kaiyō Maru*, and sailed it back to be the flagship of the Tokugawa navy. They were ordered to hand over the whole fleet to the new government but refused and sailed north, planning to set up a homeland in Ezo for the Tokugawa supporters. Nine French officers who had been training them came along.

Then the *Kaiyō Maru* sank in a huge storm. Nevertheless, the loyalists captured the town of Hakodate and declared the

Republic of Ezo. They held elections, the first ever in Japan, and elected Enomoto governor general. The American, French, and British consuls in Ezo recognized the new republic.

Back in Edo, the Americans sympathized with the Tokugawa loyalists but the British minister, Harry Parkes, gave the new government his unswerving support.

The dispute came to a head over the *Stonewall Jackson*, a formidable ironclad warship with a huge engine and walls covered in massive iron plates. It was said that whoever had her had Japan.

The shogun's government had ordered her from the Americans and paid for her. The *Stonewall* arrived in Yokohama in April 1868, but by then the shogun had been deposed and his government overthrown. The American minister resident, Robert Van Valkenburgh, wanted to give the ship to Enomoto. But Parkes reminded him of the policy of strict neutrality that Parkes himself had insisted the foreign powers adopt.

The leader of the new government, the court noble Iwakura Tomomi, promised that the ship would not be used for military purposes. Parkes relayed this to Van Valkenburgh and ordered him to hand over the ship to them.

A few days later, in direct contradiction of Iwakura's assurances, the *Stonewall* steamed north at the head of the newly formed Imperial Japanese navy.

After a fierce naval battle at Hakodate, the Tokugawa loyalists finally surrendered. Enomoto sent the navigational notes he'd brought back from Holland to the Meiji admiral so they could be of use to the country, no matter what his fate. He spent three years in prison but was pardoned and eventually rose to be navy minister in the Meiji government.

And so a new era dawned.

Japan Enters the World

CHAPTER 9

Meiji: Headlong into the Modern World

1868–1912

Examining history, we see that life has been dark and closed and that it advances in the direction of civilization and enlightenment.

Fukuzawa Yukichi, *Things Western*, 1867

Japanese look back on the men of the Meiji era as a race of heroes who engaged in epic struggles untrammeled by moral considerations, men who built empires, like the Victorians in Britain or the nineteenth-century oil and railway barons of the United States. Born after the shackles of the shogunate had fallen away, they had the taste of freedom in their mouths. The whole country lay at their feet, waiting to be conquered. The new rulers launched sweeping reforms and industrialization, shaking up society from top to bottom, aimed at turning Japan into a modern nation on a par with the West, breaking the last bonds of feudalism and swiftly transforming their country into an industrial power. By the end of the period, Japan was ready to take on Russia—and win.

CIVILIZATION AND ENLIGHTENMENT

On November 26, 1868, a splendid procession wound through the massive gates of Edo Castle with musicians stepping out in front. At the center, shouldered by sixty close-packed bearers, was the imperial palanquin topped by a golden phoenix, carrying the sixteen-year-old Emperor Mutsuhito. The imperial regalia—mirror, sword, and jewel—were carried before him.

Ten thousand people lined the streets to kneel in respectful silence as he passed. Edo was renamed Tō-kyō, "Eastern Capital," and Edo Castle became the Imperial Palace. The government declared a holiday and 2,500 casks of royal sake were distributed around the city. And right away things started to change. Japan plunged into the modern world with unprecedented speed.

Edo had been an eastern Venice, a city of canals, where people walked or went by palanquin or boat. In no time rickshaws were hurtling through the streets, drawn by runners who yelled at pedestrians to clear the way. Buildings mushroomed, built not of wood but of brick and stone. One of the first was the Tsukiji Hotel in the foreign settlement, another Mitsui House, a tiered five-story confection, built by the shopkeeping and money-exchanging Mitsui family.

With the fall of the shogunate, the lords returned to their homes in the provinces, leaving their vast Edo mansions empty. The government requisitioned the land to build ministries, barracks, and parade grounds. Tokyo became a boom town just as Edo had been under Ieyasu.

In April 1872, a backwater called the Ginza burned down. It was rebuilt with wide avenues lined with brick buildings and named Ginza Bricktown and became the new Japan's most fashionable street. It housed the newspaper office and post office and at night was lit up with Japan's first gas lamps.

That same year, the Tokyo–Yokohama line opened, designed by a British engineer with a train freighted over from

Emperor Mutsuhito opening Japan's first railway, as depicted by Charles Wirgman in The Illustrated London News, *December 21, 1872*

Britain. The emperor, now twenty, was at the sparkling new station in full court regalia to open it.

He soon set an example by changing to Western clothing, a military uniform with lots of medals, for official duties. He also made the revolutionary announcement, "I shall eat beef," upending the centuries-old Buddhist prohibition against eating meat. After having been hidden away in the imperial palace in Kyoto all these years, the emperor was now out and about, being seen by his people, who no longer even needed to put their heads in the dust when he passed.

The author and intellectual Fukuzawa Yukichi had traveled on the first Japanese missions to the United States and Europe in 1860. His books on Western manners and society were bestsellers. *Western Clothing, Food and Homes*, published in 1867, had illustrations showing how to dress, furnish your home, tell the time, and even urinate Western-style, with a picture of a chamber pot under a chest of drawers.

Men headed to the newfangled barber shops to have their topknots chopped off and their hair styled in the latest

Woodblock print artists such as Utagawa Kuniteru II were inspired by all the changes going on around them, especially the arrival of the train.

cropped cut. They tried out Western fashions—trousers, capes, horribly uncomfortable leather boots—or wore a watch in their newly discovered fob pockets, mixing and matching Japanese and Western styles with glorious abandon and showing off their new clothes at the beef restaurant, the haunt of the truly fashionable.

For the removal of the shogun was just the beginning; the changes that happened afterward were the real revolution.

The new rulers were oligarchs. They didn't have to worry about elections and could plan for the long term. Fortunately, they were also idealists and they passionately wanted to ensure Japan's survival. They deliberately and methodically reshaped society along Western lines, adopting the elements of Western culture that seemed suitable for Japan and building on the foundations that the Tokugawas had laid—the centuries of peace and stability, a well-developed merchant culture, a high level of education, a habit of duty and correct behavior, a large, hardworking workforce, and a formidable accumulation of capital.

These rulers were largely Satsuma and Chōshū samurai, headed by swashbucklers such as Saigō, Kido, and Ōkubo, who had won their spurs in the battles to topple the shogunate.

They were not bureaucrats who'd risen through the ranks or through family connections, but revolutionaries. They came to their task fresh and full of ideas. At the head were court nobles such as Iwakura Tomomi, who had done much to bring about regime change. Talented men and those with special skills were also included, even if they had sided with the shogunate.

These men had no legitimacy at all as a government; they'd arrived where they were by force of arms. But they had the emperor as a figurehead to provide the illusion of legitimacy and a sense of continuity.

The Western powers were distracted by richer and easier pickings in China and elsewhere and didn't seriously try to occupy or colonize Japan. Nevertheless, fear of colonization was a great incentive spurring the new rulers on to arm and develop fast. This was the high noon of European imperialism and it was vital to make the country strong so that it wouldn't be swallowed up like China. The way to resist the foreign powers was to fathom the secret of their military might. That meant studying their culture, learning their science and technology, and catching up with their industrial development so as to make Japan a major power equal to the West.

One urgent issue was to revoke the unequal treaties that benefited Western merchants at the expense of Japanese and exempted Westerners from Japanese justice. To do so, Japan had to persuade the West that it was as modern and Western as they, and that meant a radical overhaul of everything from the system of government to the way people dressed.

Little by little, the government lifted the restrictions that had hemmed in life. They dismantled the Tokugawa class system. People were now free to work at whatever they liked and live wherever they liked. Japanese could travel abroad and

The Iwakura mission, left to right: Kido Takayoshi, Yamaguchi Masuka, Iwakura Tomomi, Itō Hirobumi, and Ōkubo Toshimichi, 1872, San Francisco

Westerners could come to Japan. In theory at least, even out-casts became acceptable members of society.

In August 1871, Mutsuhito informed the daimyos that the 270 domains were to become prefectures, administered by Tokyo-appointed governors. The domain armies were dismantled or absorbed into the new national army.

Shortly afterward, the leading figures in the government—Iwakura, Kido, and Ōkubo—steamed off on an eighteen-month tour of the United States and Europe. The plan was to introduce the new regime to foreign governments, try to revise the unequal treaties, and learn the secrets of Western industrialization firsthand.

In the United States, they visited schools, industrial plants, workshops, vineyards, and California gold mines; in Britain shipyards, iron and steel works, railways, and coal mines. They were excited to learn that most of these developments had happened over the last forty or fifty years. Surely Japan, too, could industrialize with equal speed. Christianity, they noticed, provided a spiritual backbone for Western civilization. Perhaps the emperor and Shinto could provide a similar symbolic foundation for Japan. The watchword was to be "Japanese spirit, Western learning."

Back home, they hired highly qualified foreign experts, paying them huge salaries to introduce new technology, share their knowledge, and train a new generation of Japanese specialists. Engineers, technicians, military consultants, teachers, and financial and legal advisers all arrived. Nearly half were British and the rest German, French, Dutch, and American. Within a few years, there were the beginnings of a telegraph system, the first lighthouses, a postal service, compulsory education at primary school level encouraging Western-style individualistic thinking, and Western-style law courts. The Western calendar was adopted, the first modern library built, and the first daily newspaper published.

To finance the new Japan, Shibusawa Eichi, the "father of Japanese capitalism," founded Japan's first modern bank with the help of the huge family-run conglomerates of Sumitomo, Mitsui, Mitsubishi, and Yasuda, who provided the financial underpinning for business and industry. As head of the tax bureau, he instituted tax reform, to be paid not in rice but in cash. He aimed to transform the image of the merchants from low-ranking parasites to vital members of society who made money in order to fund the necessary developments.

In the early years, Japan's main industry was textiles and its main export silk. Young rural women operated imported silk-reeling machines under Dickensian conditions. Western-style clothing needed wool and this, too, stimulated the development of the textile industry. Later, the country moved increasingly into manufacturing and heavy industry and by the end of the period was a major world shipbuilder. The government also began to lay out a communications network of roads, bridges, and ports.

But not everyone benefited from this brave new Japan or was happy with it.

THE LAST SAMURAI

Samurai in particular were outraged by the overturning of the old order. When the domain armies were disbanded, they found themselves unemployed, while universal conscription meant that peasants now carried weapons, an intolerable humiliation. There was a rash of uprisings against the destruction of the old way of life.

The opposition coalesced around the charismatic figure of Saigō, who had led the revolutionary armies and negotiated the handover of Edo Castle. He was now councillor of the realm and commander in chief of the armed forces but still wore homespun kimonos and straw sandals.

When the Iwakura mission went to Europe and the United States, he stayed to run the government. When problems arose over Korea, he made plans to go to war, to give work to unemployed samurai. The Iwakura mission rushed back just in time to veto them.

In disgust he resigned and went back to Satsuma, where he established schools, effectively a private army. The last straw was when the government forbade samurai to carry swords or wear the topknot and deprived them of their rice stipends. Saigō agreed to lead a march on Tokyo, sure that disaffected samurai all over the country would join him.

In February 1877, he led an army of seven thousand north toward the great fortress at Kumamoto. The commander refused them passage and Saigō settled down to besiege it. It was a crucial mistake. It gave the government time to ship its forces down to Kyushu. There was a huge battle and five thousand Satsuma were killed. Saigō and the remnants of his army set off around Kyushu, dodging government troops.

On September 22, 1877, he was hiding out in a cave with just three hundred men and no ammunition. Before dawn, the imperial army, thirty thousand strong, closed in. Saigō and forty men charged down the hill, swords drawn. Saigō was hit in the groin by a bullet. He turned to Beppu Shinsuke, his appointed second, and said, "Shin, my good friend, here is as good as anywhere." Beppu cut off his head and shouted that the master was dead. The remaining men rushed toward enemy lines and were mown down by rifle fire.

Saigō was widely mourned and has gone down in history as the last samurai. And so ended the last attempt to resist the spread of Westernization in Japan.

DANCING FOR THE COUNTRY

In 1883, a grand Italianate mansion with colonnaded verandas opened in central Tokyo. Set in landscaped gardens and designed by the British architect Josiah Conder, it was called the Rokumeikan, Deer Cry Hall. Here gentlemen in frock coats and ladies in bustles, corsets, and bonnets dined on French food cooked by French chefs, played billiards, had charity bazaars, played the piano, and sang Western songs.

At the balls, gentlemen were supposed to appear with their wives on their arms, like Westerners. But Japanese wives were not used to going out with their husbands, let alone dancing, and many of the ladies were geisha, not wives.

The Rokumeikan seemed to embody the new Japan. By now Itō Hirobumi, the Chōshū man who had burned down the British legation and studied in London in the 1860s, was prime minister. He was a bon vivant who loved playing host at geisha parties. The pinnacle of decadence came when he threw a masked ball, dressed as a Venetian nobleman, and seduced the wife of one of his councillors. His cabinet became known as "the dancing cabinet," and shortly afterward he fell from power. It was the moment when the love affair with Western fashions turned sour.

Ōkubo had been the most powerful figure in the government. To demonstrate that clan loyalties were over, he personally led the troops that put down Saigō's rebellion. Shortly afterward, he was assassinated by outraged Satsuma samurai. Kido, too, had died and a younger generation of leaders emerged with Itō as the leading statesman.

Japanese negotiators continued to meet their Western counterparts but the unequal treaties remained unchanged. All the undignified aping of Western ways hadn't done the trick. People began to feel a renewed pride in traditional Japanese values and culture. Women put away their bustles and bonnets and went back to kimonos. New editions of works by Saikaku, Chikamatsu, and Bashō came out alongside Western-influenced works by contemporary Japanese writers.

A major irritant was the stranglehold that the men of Satsuma and Chōshū had over the government. Men from other rebel domains, such as Itagaki Taisuke, a thin-faced swashbuckler from Tosa who had led the assault on Aizu Castle, began to assert themselves.

In 1875, Itagaki launched the Freedom and People's Rights Movement. He called for a national assembly, a written constitution, and an elected legislature and demanded that the people—meaning men above a certain income—be given a voice in political affairs. He made rabble-rousing speeches up and down the country and produced pamphlets, books, and newspapers agitating for democratic reform. The movement spread right down to the former outcast class.

There were demonstrations and rioting just as Saigō was leading his rebellion. The government hurriedly issued laws clamping down on freedom of speech and association. Finally, in 1881, they issued an imperial edict promising a constitution and a national parliament by 1890. Itagaki formed the Liberal Party in preparation for the new day.

Ōkuma Shigenobu, a stern bulldog of a man from Saga, had been one of the last non-Satsuma Chōshū statesmen in the government. He too was a radical with a swashbuckling past, an outsider up against the establishment. He formed the Progressive Party, demanding a British-style parliamentary system.

Both leaders were charismatic figures who lived their lives in public and were under threat. Itagaki was stabbed by a would-be assassin and shouted the legendary words, "Itagaki may die but freedom never!" Ōkuma, who had reentered the government as foreign minister, lost a leg when a right-wing nationalist threw a bomb into his carriage, enraged by the failure yet again to get rid of the hated unequal treaties. When he was convalescing, he joked that the loss of his leg meant there was more blood to circulate to his brain.

The government kept its word. Itō went to Europe to study constitutional systems and in 1885 formed the first cabinet, with himself as prime minister.

On February 11, 1889, the anniversary of the founding of the empire of Japan by the legendary first emperor, Jimmu, in 660 BCE, there was a huge parade to celebrate the new constitution with the emperor and empress, in Western dress, at the center. The constitution provided for a diet (parliament) with two chambers, a House of Peers and a House of Representatives, elected by a limited franchise. The diet, however, had no real powers and could not appoint ministers of state. Actual power lay with the cabinet, made up of the Satsuma Chōshū leaders who had been running Japan all along. There was also a privy council of elder statesmen to advise the cabinet on matters of major importance. The underpinning of the whole edifice, embodying the power of the state, was the emperor, descended from a line of sovereigns "unbroken for ages eternal," a unique and sacrosanct institution. Despite all these qualifications, it was a huge step forward, and in 1890, Japan's first-ever national elections were held for the new diet.

The Japanese had modernized and industrialized with amazing speed, within the space of a generation. But meanwhile, the imperial powers had been closing in. The barbarians were at the gates.

A DINER AT THE TABLE

In July 1894, the Japanese were attacking Seonghwan Fort in Korea. Bugler Shirakami Genjirō's commanding officer ordered him to sound the charge. As he sounded it, he was struck by a bullet. With his last breath, he raised his bugle and sounded it again before falling dead.

His heroism struck a chord back home and he was immortalized in poems, plays, songs, and woodblock prints.

Bugler Shirakami sounds his last note, note, as depicted in Japanese Spirit
by Ōkura Kōtō, January 12, 1894.

After its devastating defeats in the Opium Wars, Japan's giant
neighbor, Qing-dynasty China, was at the mercy of Britain,
France, and Russia and forced to consume Britain's opium.
Meanwhile, Nikolai II's Russia was expanding its vast empire
eastward, completing the Trans-Siberian railway to Vladivostok,
determined to control the warm-water harbor of Port Arthur at
the tip of the Liaotung Peninsula as its gateway to the Pacific.

At the start of the Meiji period, Japan had not had the military might or economic strength to stand up to such overwhelming power. For twenty years, the policy had been to avoid confrontation with the West. But now the government focused on protecting the country against invasion and colonization and on finally having the unequal treaties rescinded.

From the start, they had made the army and navy the priority and devoted a third of the national budget to them. Initially the army was developed on the French model with French advisers, as it had been under Yoshinobu. Then in 1871, after France's defeat in the Franco-Prussian War, the government brought in Prussian advisers and reshaped the army on the German model, making it more mobile and better organized and drilled. In 1873, they introduced universal conscription. The newly upgraded imperial army soon showed its mettle, putting down peasant revolts and samurai uprisings such as the Satsuma Rebellion. By the 1890s, it was equipped with modern rifles and artillery, mostly manufactured in Japan, and was the equal of any European army. The imperial navy was modeled on the British navy with an officers' training school and a small fleet.

Japan had begun to expand its borders. In 1869, it absorbed the northern island of Ezo, home to the Ainu people, where the Tokugawa loyalists had established their short-lived republic, and renamed it Hokkaido. Japanese settlers, including unemployed samurai, colonized and developed the land. In 1879, Japan took over the Ryukyu kingdom and renamed it Okinawa Prefecture.

The big worry was Korea, the Hermit Kingdom, which was simply too close for comfort. Trouble had been simmering with China over Korea for years. The Qing rulers claimed the

Hermit Kingdom as a protectorate, while Japan asserted that it was an independent country, certainly not a vassal of China. For Japan, control of Korea was vital to national security. Only under "enlightened" Japanese influence rather than the patronage of a much-weakened China could Korea withstand the predatory threat of the Western colonizers. Japan also needed a foothold on the continent to boost its economic prosperity.

In 1894, peasant unrest in Korea blew up into a huge uprising. The Korean king called on China to help and China sent in forces. Japan, too, sent in troops, aiming to establish a pro-reform and pro-Japanese government. Japanese forces seized the royal palace and on August 1 declared war on China.

China's army and navy were much larger than Japan's, but Japan's were better equipped and better trained. To the amazement of the watching Western world, within a couple of months the Japanese army had taken most of Korea in a series of quick and easy victories with relatively few casualties and the navy had command of the Yellow Sea, between China and Korea. By February 1895, they had advanced into southern Manchuria and the Liaotung Peninsula, including Port Arthur.

Finally, they negotiated a ceasefire. The Japanese government demanded an indemnity, the handing over of Liaotung and Taiwan, which they had not even occupied, and a commercial treaty giving Japan the same trading privileges as the Western powers had in China. The Treaty of Shimonoseki established Japan as the paramount power in East Asia and made Korea independent of China. The West saw it as a David and Goliath victory, the tiny island nation of Japan against the Chinese giant, and that year finally repealed the unequal treaties.

The Japanese were exultant. But, as the government knew, the terms depended on the agreement of the Western powers. Russia in particular saw the Liaotung Peninsula as a crucial link in its own route to China by way of Manchuria.

A month after the victory, the Russian, French, and German representatives in Tokyo "advised" the Japanese government to return the Liaotung Peninsula to China so as to maintain peace in Asia. Japan was not strong enough to resist. This Triple Intervention was a bitter reminder that Japan was still at the mercy of the Western powers.

The government took a step back. They increased the size of the army, made the country self-sufficient in military equipment and manufacturing facilities, and greatly increased the navy. Thus, the war accelerated the development of heavy industries such as shipbuilding and railways.

The war with Japan had made China's weakness painfully obvious. The predatory Western powers hovered, waiting to pounce. In 1898, Britain, Russia, and Germany had completed their "scramble for Africa" and set about "carving the Chinese melon." The country that took the largest slice was Russia, which, adding insult to injury, "leased" the Liaotung Peninsula, the very peninsula that it had denied Japan in the interests of Asian peace. After the Boxer Rebellion of 1899 to 1900—when the Boxer militia, a movement of thousands of dissatisfied Chinese youths, unsuccessfully tried to drive the foreigners out of China—Russia seized most of Manchuria on the pretext that the Boxers threatened railway installations there.

In 1902, the Japanese negotiated the Anglo-Japanese alliance to prevent any further Russian advance, ensuring that Japan would have the protection of one of the great powers against the others. It was the first alliance between a Western and a non-Western nation as equal signatories.

By the beginning of 1904, tensions between Russia and Japan had come to a head over the question of Korea. With Russia building a second track for the Trans-Siberian Railway, there was a chance that Russia might use its huge strength in Manchuria to invade Japan. For its own security, Japan had to eject Russia from Manchuria. It was time to face off against a Western nation.

On February 8, 1904, the Imperial Japanese Navy launched a surprise attack on the Russian fleet at Port Arthur at the tip of the Laiotung Peninsula. Having bottled up the surviving Russian ships in the harbor, they landed troops to drive the Russians out of Manchuria. There were very heavy casualties on both sides. The Russian commander at Port Arthur unexpectedly surrendered at the beginning of January 1905, to the surprise of the Japanese.

Meanwhile, the huge Russian Baltic Fleet had sailed around Africa and Asia to break the blockade of Vladivostok, only to be decimated by the Imperial Japanese Navy at the Battle of Tsushima in May 1905. Western newspapers applauded as "Gallant Little Japan Stands Up to the Russian Bear." The British were so impressed they gave a lock of Nelson's hair to the Imperial Japanese Navy, declaring that its victory was as great as Nelson's at Trafalgar.

In actuality, Japan never expected to win the war. It hoped just to force Russia to enter negotiations to be chaired by President Theodore Roosevelt. The scholar and government minister Kaneko Kentarō, who had studied at Harvard Law School and was a personal friend of Roosevelt's, had gone back to the United States to arrange for Roosevelt to mediate.

The Treaty of Portsmouth was signed in September 1905. Russia recognized Japan's freedom of action in Korea and Japan took over the lease of Liaotung, but Russia was not required to pay an indemnity. The Japanese public had expected more and there were riots. Nevertheless, Japan was finally recognized as a world power—a diner at the table, not part of the meal.

Shortly afterward, Japan made Korea a Japanese protectorate, backed by its Western allies who saw it as justifiable protection against potential Russian aggression. Itō, a grand old man by now, was posted to Seoul as resident-general. Japan enjoyed railway, mining, and fishery rights, along with timber concessions, and land was made available for Japanese settlers. Korean dissidents rose up in fury, and in 1909 a Korean patriot shot and killed Itō.

Itō's last word was, "Fool!" He knew that his death would damage, not help, Korea. He was right. The following year, Japan took Korea as a Japanese colony.

On July 29, 1912, Emperor Mutsuhito died. The funeral took place at night. People traveled from the farthest parts of Japan to bow in silent respect as the imperial hearse rolled by, drawn by five oxen, attended by traditional coffin bearers, and followed by a seemingly endless cortege, some in ancient court costume, others in military uniform. Cannons thundered and temple bells tolled. The black lacquer wheels of the ox cart reflected torch and arc lights. The body was taken by slow train to Kyoto, where a hundred men carried the coffin to the mausoleum.

The era of giants who had transformed the country was over. No one knew what the future had in store, but it certainly looked bright.

Japan Meets the West

While Japanese experimented with bustles, bonnets, and beef, on the other side of the world, Westerners were discovering a new and enchanting culture. In 1858, after Japan opened to trade with the West, Japanese goods suddenly became widely available. Poverty-stricken samurai sold their heirlooms, often at reduced prices, and swords, helmets, armor, kimonos, and exquisite porcelain found their way into the curio shops of the West.

Everyone was intrigued and charmed by the delicacy, precision, and beauty of Japanese art and artifacts. Trendsetting women wore kimonos, fashionable people collected woodblock prints, and filled their homes with screens, fans, lacquerware, blue-and-white porcelain, vases, curved swords, netsuke, and artifacts inspired by Japanese art. Audiences flocked to see Japan-inspired plays and operas, from *The Geisha* with Marie Tempest to Gilbert and Sullivan's *The Mikado* and David Belasco's play *Madame Butterfly*, which opened in March 1900 and inspired Puccini's *Madama Butterfly*.

Japonisme, as the craze was dubbed, swept the West, inspiring artists, architects, and interior designers and spawning Art Nouveau. In 1856, the artist Félix Bracquemond discovered a collection of manga engravings by Hokusai in Paris (*manga* simply means "whimsical drawing," the same term used for manga comics today) and soon a generation of Western artists were collecting, being inspired by, and sometimes copying Japanese woodblock prints. In 1876, Monet painted his wife

Camille in an extraordinary Japanese kimono. Van Gogh had six hundred woodblock prints and wrote that he yearned to visit Japan or at least learn to see with Japanese eyes.

Meanwhile, Japanese were eager to visit the West. In 1866, the government lifted the prohibition against foreign travel and issued the first "letters of request." Officially, the idea was for diplomats, government officials, merchants, and students to go abroad to help develop Japan and its economy. But entertainers were also eager to see the world.

Among the first was a legendary juggler and spinner of tops called Matsui Gensui XIII. The Gensui troupe made their debut to a packed house at St. Martin's Hall, just behind the Royal Opera House in Covent Garden, in London, in 1867. They toured England, performed for the royal family at Windsor Castle, and appeared at the 1867 Paris Expo.

To the Victorians, Japan's most visible representatives were its acrobats and stage performers, and in his *Around the World in Eighty Days*, Jules Verne depicted Japan as a land of acrobats.

CHAPTER 10

Taishō: Crosscurrents
1912–1926

The Taishō era was Japan's Jazz Age. A new generation had arrived whose parents had never known life under the shogunate and who looked to the West for ideas and inspiration. The air fizzed with words such as socialism and Marxism, anarchism, democracy, and freedom. It was, said one writer, the age of speed, sport, and sex. But there were darker undertones. The right wing and the military fiercely opposed all these radical ideas and had opinions of their own on the way Japan should be going.

TAISHŌ DEMOCRACY

At the first state opening of the Imperial Diet, after the accession of Yoshihito, whose posthumous name was Taishō, "Great Righteousness," the members gathered in respectful silence to hear the new emperor's maiden speech. A mustachioed man of thirty-four, resplendent in a military uniform bedecked with medals, Yoshihito gazed around at them. Time passed. He was still staring. The members fidgeted nervously. Who dared stand up and prompt the Son of Heaven?

Then he began to laugh uproariously. He rolled up his speech, put it to his eye, and squinted around at the august gathering.

Yoshihito was the first of Mutsuhito's sons to survive. As a boy, he had had meningitis. People said he was mad. After that memorable diet appearance, he was kept well out of the public eye.

It was clear that the Taishō period was going to be very different from the heroic Meiji era. The aging Satsuma and Chōshū samurai who ruled the country had controlled every part of the government—the ministries, the armed forces, the cabinet, and the diet. They had done so through Mutsuhito as a symbol of unquestionable authority. But with his death, this cozy arrangement began to fall apart. Many of the elder statesmen were now dead. The military was growing in power and there were regular disagreements between it and the civilian government.

Meanwhile, the diet was finding its teeth. There had been elections, though these were limited to the wealthiest 3 percent of the population. The ruling samurai had assumed such men would be docile, but more than half voted for opposition parties. Although the diet had no power, its members were able to obstruct every government bill, and there were stormy scenes.

Finally, the cabinet called in a man who was outside of the political infighting—the much-respected and popular Ōkuma Shigenobu, who had had his leg blown off by a nationalist. He became prime minister in April 1914 at the age of seventy-six.

It seemed a sign of hope. At last, the Satsuma Chōshū stranglehold had been loosened. Perhaps Ōkuma would lead a Taishō revolution as far-reaching as the Meiji revolution had been.

On the other side of the world, the Great War had broken out. For Japan, it was too good an opportunity to miss. When

Britain asked for assistance in destroying the German navy in and around Chinese waters, the Ōkuma cabinet issued an ultimatum to Germany to remove their ships and declared war when the ultimatum was ignored. Japan promptly snapped up the German colonies in China and the north Pacific.

With Europe engulfed in war, there was limitless demand from Japan's European allies for ships and munitions and, with Western businesses turned over to a war footing, civilian goods as well. The war disrupted European supply chains and markets in the Far East, and Africa suddenly opened to Japanese goods. For Japan, thousands of miles away from the fighting, the war was a bonanza, enabling it to build up its heavy industry and diversify manufacturing. Between 1913 and 1918, exports quadrupled. Many companies—from the *zaibatsu*, huge family-run conglomerates such as Mitsui and Sumitomo, to small manufacturing and financial concerns—made fortunes. The prosperity spread across the country.

Just as the Western powers had carved the Chinese melon, Japan, too, had taken a slice. For the West, China was on the other side of the world, but for Japan it was strategically all-important. In 1912, the last Manchu emperor, Puyi, had been forced to abdicate and a revolutionary government came into power under General Yuan Shih-k'ai. Now, with Europe in upheaval, it was a good opportunity to assert Japan's power and influence over its large but weak and chaotic neighbor.

Japan had already taken Korea, established a presence in Manchuria through the Portsmouth Treaty, and occupied the German colonies in China. In 1915, Ōkuma's foreign minister presented a list of Twenty-One Demands to Yuan Shih-k'ai to allow Japanese companies to do business, own land, carry out mining, and extend the Japanese-owned railway system in Manchuria and Outer Mongolia. He also demanded that China buy half its arms from Japan and take on Japanese military advisers, effectively turning China into a Japanese protectorate. Yuan was forced to sign most of the clauses.

When the war came to an end in 1918, Japan sent the suave French-speaking aristocrat Saionji Kinmochi as its chief delegate to the peace conference at Versailles. He sat alongside Britain, France, Italy, and the United States, marking Japan as one of the great powers. Japan became a founding member of the League of Nations. But Saionji was unable to have the League of Nations' charter include a racial equality clause, which was opposed by the United States and Australia, both segregated countries. Nevertheless, the treaty recognized Japan's possession of the former German territories in China.

With the Great War ended, the age of the masses arrived. On the streets, young Japanese were fired up by news of the 1917 Russian Revolution and even more by the Bolshevik Revolution. Many started learning Russian, and there were eager converts to liberalism, socialism, anarchism, and other left-wing movements. Many more began to question the established order in Japan. The great new powers were America, the land of democracy, and Russia, the inspiring new communist state.

The lower orders had tasted freedom for the first time only fifty years earlier. Now their children's children were discovering what it meant.

Japan's economic boom led to surging inflation. In 1918, the price of rice, the staple food, soared, but government regulation ensured that the amount farmers received remained the same. Rents and the prices of goods in shops shot up. House-wives and farmers mobilized, unleashing a torrent of anger that spread across Japan.

There were peaceful protests, then strikes and riots. In Tokyo, marauding bands ranged through the city, burning and looting. There were pitched battles between tens of thousands of rioters and the police, and the army had to be called in.

Itō Hirobumi had founded a political party, the Seiyūkai, Association of Political Friends. The most prominent member was Hara Takashi, an indomitable campaigner for party rule. Not only was he outside the Satsuma Chōshū clique, he was also a Catholic and a canny operator. While many of the elder statesmen had taken titles—Itō, for example, became Prince Itō—Hara remained stubbornly a commoner and took on the mantle of representative of the people. When the government fell as a result of the rice riots, he became prime minister. For the first time, Japan was under the rule of an elected representative of the people. The Taishō era, it seemed, was to be the age of democracy.

Hara filled his cabinet with members of his own party. But there was not much in the way of reform. Socialist thought was ruthlessly suppressed, corruption was ignored, and there was no move toward universal suffrage.

THE ROARING TWENTIES

Unlike Meiji times, when "civilization and enlightenment" had been restricted to the wealthy and privileged, by the 1920s, the spread of mass culture affected nearly everyone in Japan. For many people, this was a time of hope and exhilaration. There was an intoxication with everything that seemed

Moga *were liberated women, flappers who drank, smoked, and practiced free love.*

to symbolize the new age. Men built railways and bridges, carved out manufacturing empires, imported and exported anything that would sell. They opened banks, they dealt in stocks and shares.

Buses, trams, and cars, mainly imported American ones, rattled around streets festooned with telegraph and electric cables and lined with shops and glossy department stores full of enticing goods. The grandest store was Mitsukoshi, the retail arm of the vast Mitsui business empire, where intellectuals, writers, and "people of culture" met to observe and discuss.

There was universal education. Tokyo had one of the world's largest student populations. The high rates of literacy led to a boom in book, journal, and newspaper publishing. People were free to think and talk and argue. They even had money and could spend it as crazily as they liked.

It was the age of anything goes. The trendsetters were *moga* ("modern gals") and *mobo* ("modern boys"). *Moga* cut their hair as short as boys and flaunted short flapper skirts, a far cry from the modest kimono. Dapper *mobo* wore their hair long and combed straight back and sported bell bottoms, bowler hats, and horn-rimmed Harold Lloyd glasses.

They hung out in cafes and bars; they smoked, talked, and argued; they practiced free love and they strolled up and down the Ginza. They listened to jazz, danced the Charleston, watched American movies, and ate ice cream. Until the authorities clamped down, Marxism was all the rage, and everyone read the latest revolutionary Russian novels.

Cosmopolitan Japan was high on the international circuit. In 1918, Sergei Prokofiev gave a recital tour and Anna Pavlova performed her "Dying Swan" to enraptured audiences, and in 1922, Albert Einstein spent two months in Japan, which he found fascinating, exotic, and somewhat hard to understand.

Then, just before noon on Saturday, September 1, 1923, disaster struck. As charcoal braziers were burning under the midday meal across Tokyo, there was a violent shockwave. Within minutes the city was in ruins. The brick-built Asakusa

The Asakusa Twelve Stories, Japan's first skyscraper, symbolized modern Tokyo. It was damaged in the earthquake of 1923 and was never rebuilt.

Twelve Stories, which had towered over the east end, was severely damaged; temples collapsed under their heavy roofs; wooden houses tumbled like packs of cards.

Then came firestorms, lit by the braziers. The city blazed uncontrollably for nearly two days. More than 130,000 people died and 2.5 million lost their homes. The great city of Tokyo—with its universities, tram lines, and avenues lined with willows—was reduced to a plain of rubble. A few skeletal buildings remained, tottering above the ruins.

The Great Kanto Earthquake is etched into the memory of every Japanese person. Many fled the city. Those who remained had to stand in line for hours for a single rice ball. People searched frantically among the ruins for lost relatives. There was looting and rioting. In the aftermath, rumors spread blaming Koreans for poisoning wells. Soldiers, police, and vigilantes took advantage of the chaos to kill six thousand Koreans and left-wing activists.

The earthquake marked the definitive end of old Edo. The city was rebuilt as quickly as possible, with many more Western-style brick and stone buildings. Streets were widened, though the street pattern remained similar to that of Edo. There were big new parks and even more bars, cafes, movie theaters, and dance halls where people could meet and socialize. And soon Taishō democracy and the Jazz Age were in full swing again.

Yoshihito's son, Hirohito, had become regent after his father became incapable of carrying out his official duties. A few months after the earthquake, as he was traveling past the Tiger Gate intersection, a student fired a pistol at his carriage. At his trial, the would-be assassin yelled, "Long live the Communist Party of Japan!"

By the 1924 election, the opposition parties were strong enough to make a serious bid for power. That May, a coalition became the new ruling party. The following year, all men over the age of twenty-five were finally given the vote, quadrupling the size of the electorate. It was the pinnacle of Taishō democracy. Yet only a week later, the same parliament passed the Peace Preservation Law, giving the police new powers to clamp down on left-wing groups.

In December 1926, Yoshihito died of pneumonia and was buried the following February with suitable reverence and pageantry in the western suburbs of Tokyo. The traditional coffin bearers came down from Kyoto by train, bringing the imperial coffin with them. Yoshihito had been the first Tokyo emperor, born and buried in Tokyo.

And so Hirohito ascended the Chrysanthemum Throne.

Many great writers tackled the contradictions of life in this strange and rather thrilling new world. Novelists such as

Natsume Sōseki, Nagai Kafū, and Tanizaki Jun'ichirō wrote of the wrenching loss of the old ways and the convolutions that people went through as they tried to come to terms with the new.

But there were already dark undertones. The army was out of control and there were many who disapproved of the way that society was going: the liberalism, the permissiveness, the infatuation with left-wing ideologies. The future no longer seemed so bright.

Pioneering Feminists

The Taishō period was a great time to be a woman. While Meiji society had required women to fit the template of "good wife, wise mother," young Taishō women could choose to be typists, elevator girls, shop clerks, nurses, beauticians, journalists, or writers and make themselves financially independent. Some *moga* worked as waitresses in cafes, dispensing sexual favors where they saw fit. The ultimate *moga* was Naomi in Tanizaki Jun'ichirō's novel *A Fool's Love*, the story of a man hopelessly besotted with one of these cool, aloof creatures.

Some women were prepared to speak up for their rights. In 1911, Hiratsuka Raichō founded *Seitō* (*Bluestocking*)—Japan's first all-women literary magazine. The first words were "In the beginning woman was the sun," referring to Amaterasu, the Sun Goddess. With its stories freely expressing women's sexuality, the magazine shocked and outraged the upholders of traditional values. But what really infuriated the government were its articles criticizing the established capitalist order.

In 1916, the Home Ministry forbade distributors to supply the magazine and it closed down.

Hiratsuka was the ultimate Taishō woman. She eloped with a married man and had two children by a younger lover, whom she married only when the children were adults.

Seitō's most famous contributor was the poet Yosano Akiko. She, too, had an affair with a married man whom she later married, and her first volume of poems, *Midaregami* ("Tangled Hair"), was a passionate love letter to him. At the height of the Russo-Japanese War, she published a poem titled "Thou Shalt Not Die," exhorting her brother who was a soldier not to sacrifice himself for a senseless war. It became the anthem of the anti-war movement and was taken up again after World War II.

Japan in the Twentieth and Twenty-First Centuries

CHAPTER 11

Shōwa: From Defeat to Prosperity
1926–1989

The Shōwa ("Enlightened Peace") era, the reign of Emperor Hirohito, spanned most of the twentieth century. It began with the worst disaster Japan has ever faced, the years of militarism that Japanese of the time called the Dark Valley, followed by the devastation of the war, and ended with unprecedented prosperity. The 1980s were the years of the "bubble economy," when the West feared that Japan was taking over the world. Awash in money, the Japanese created extraordinary fashions, arts, and buildings, and Tokyo blossomed into one of the most glamorous cities on earth.

THE DARK VALLEY

On May 14, 1932, Charlie Chaplin arrived in Kobe, eager to see "the land of cherry blossoms." Thousands crowded to greet him and airplanes flew low scattering pamphlets of welcome.

The next day, Takeru, the son of the prime minister, Inukai Tsuyoshi, took Chaplin to a sumo tournament. In the middle of a match, a messenger arrived. Takeru returned to his seat looking ashen. He covered his face with his hands and said, "My father has just been assassinated." Chaplin later discovered that the assassins had intended to kill him, too, thinking that would bring about war with America.

On the surface, life may have seemed much as before. But even a celebrity such as Charlie Chaplin could not avoid brushing up against the increasing unrest.

Western nations watched Japan's incursions into China with growing concern. In 1921, the Washington Naval Conference terminated the Anglo-Japanese Alliance and barred Japan from having navies as large as those of Britain and the United States. America passed an Immigration Act specifically excluding Japanese immigrants. The United States already had a plan for possible confrontation with Japan—War Plan Orange, operating out of American bases in Hawaii, Guam, and the Philippines.

In the worldwide stock market crash of 1929, many Japanese people lost their jobs and rice prices plummeted. Japan had few natural resources and had to import oil, iron, steel, and other commodities for its industries and military. To generate the currency to buy these, it exported mainly tea, machinery, and textiles such as raw silk; but other nations imposed tariffs to protect their own struggling businesses and Japanese exports fell by half. In times of hardship, Western nations fell back on their colonies. Japan needed to do the same, to increase the amount of territory from which it could obtain raw materials. That meant tapping the resources of China.

Without informing their superiors, some junior officers in the Kwangtung Army, which guarded the South Manchurian Railway and Japanese holdings in Manchuria, set off bombs on the railway outside Mukden. They claimed that the perpetrators were Chinese dissidents, which gave the army a pretext to invade Manchuria.

Six months later, they had taken Southern Manchuria, declared it an independent state, and named it Manchukuo.

The plan was to turn it into an industrial powerhouse to supply the Japanese empire. Puyi, the last Manchu emperor, was installed as a puppet ruler.

The League of Nations refused to recognize Manchukuo and condemned Japan as an aggressor, and in 1933 Japan formally withdrew from the League.

Prime Minister Inukai's assassination marked the end of democracy in Japan. Thereafter, the army chose the cabinet. Anyone who opposed them risked assassination. Communists, communist sympathizers, and people suspected of being communist sympathizers were arrested and put in prison, mainly without trial, and some were tortured. Thought control spread to books and newspapers, then to anything that smacked of the West. Jazz was suspect. Finally, the dancing had to stop.

People took refuge from the sense of impending cataclysm in escapist entertainment—*ero guro nansensu*, "erotic, grotesque nonsense," a blackly humorous fascination with everything that was weird and off-kilter. They threw themselves into hedonistic pleasures as if there was no tomorrow—as indeed there might not be. The heart of the decadence was the Casino Folies in Asakusa, Tokyo's wild East End, the haunt of gangsters, dancers, and assorted lowlifes. There crowds gathered to watch erotic revues. The writer Kawabata Yasunari's *The Scarlet Gang of Asakusa*, full of *ero*, *guro*, and *nansensu*, is set there. He would go on to win Japan's first Nobel Prize in Literature.

The person who most embodied the mood of the times was Abe Sada, who strangled her lover in an erotic game and carried his penis in her kimono sleeve until she was apprehended. Crowds poured in to her trial and there was massive press coverage. Her story is told in Ōshima Nagisa's sexually explicit movie *Ai no Corrida* (*In the Realm of the Senses*).

But no matter how much people tried to bury themselves in distractions, it was harder and harder to ignore the perilous direction in which the country was going.

THE ARMY UNLEASHED

One hot July day in 1937, at Marco Polo Bridge just outside Peking (Beijing), a Japanese private went missing. The Japanese troops, who were nose to nose with the Chinese army there, demanded to enter the town to search for him, and when the Chinese refused, there was an exchange of fire. Thus, Japan blundered into war with China—though it's possible that the whole incident was engineered by the Japanese military.

Once the fighting started, it quickly escalated into an unstoppable conflict between the Japanese army and the Kuomintang, the Chinese National Revolutionary Army, led by General Chiang Kai-shek. The Japanese captured Peking, then marched on the cosmopolitan city of Shanghai. Chiang retreated up the Yangtze to his capital, Nanking (Nanjing). When the Japanese arrived at the fortified walls, Chiang and most of his government flew to safety, leaving Chinese troops to mount a brief defense before the Japanese broke through.

Hirohito's uncle, Prince Asaka Yasuhiko, flew in from Tokyo to take command, with orders to ensure the city's subjugation. He issued the fateful order: "Kill all captives."

Nanking was captured after five days. Then Japanese soldiers went on a rampage. For three months, they committed terrible atrocities, raping, looting, committing arson, torturing, and murdering between two hundred thousand and three hundred thousand Chinese prisoners of war and civilians. The soldiers were mainly reservists, conscripts fresh from the rice fields, untrained and left to fend for themselves. There were not enough military policemen to maintain order and many of the younger officers belonged to right-wing ultranationalist groups. As F. Tillman Durdin, who witnessed the first days of the massacres, wrote in *The New York Times* on December 18, 1937, the rape of Nanking "will remain a blot on the reputation of the Japanese army and nation."

The capture of Nanking did not lead to Chinese surrender. No matter how many cities the Japanese took, Chiang Kai-shek simply retreated deeper and deeper into the hinterland and carried on fighting.

What drove the Japanese advance was the need for raw materials. As the army moved south in search of oil and other resources, the prime minister, the aristocratic, right-leaning Prince Konoe Fumimaro, announced the formation of the Greater East Asia Co-Prosperity Sphere, an economically self-sufficient zone under the command of Japan, incorporating Southeast Asia and eventually Australia and New Zealand—effectively a Japanese empire.

In September 1939, war broke out in Europe. By summer 1940, Germany had occupied France, Holland, and Belgium, and Britain seemed on the brink of surrender, leaving the Asian colonies of Britain, France, and Holland undefended and ripe for the picking. In September 1940, Japan signed the Tripartite Pact with Germany and Italy.

Less than a year later, Japanese troops were marching through the jungles of French Indochina. The United States, followed by Britain, imposed a trade embargo, cutting Japan's lifeline to vital oil supplies and demanding that the Japanese withdraw not only from Indochina but also from China.

By now, Japan was desperately short of oil, rubber, tin, and other raw materials. There was only enough fuel to supply the armed forces and the domestic economy for a few more weeks. Konoe proposed a personal meeting with President Franklin D. Roosevelt to find a solution to the differences between the US and Japan, but Roosevelt refused.

Unable to break the deadlock, Konoe and his cabinet resigned. His successor was the war minister, General "Razor" Tōjō Hideki, a militant right-winger.

With Tōjō in power, war was inevitable. On the morning of December 7, 1941, the Japanese launched a surprise attack on Pearl Harbor and other bases from which the British and Americans could intercept their planned assault on Southeast Asia. Three hundred and fifty Japanese fighters, bombers, and torpedo planes destroyed nearly two hundred American planes and sank four battleships, killing more than 2,400 military personnel. Japan also issued a declaration of war, but it did not arrive until after the attack.

Within the first days, most of America's air and sea forces in the Pacific were destroyed or immobilized. Japan took Hong Kong, Singapore, the Philippines, Malaya, the Dutch East Indies, and Burma, along with thousands of prisoners of war. At first, the Japanese were welcomed as liberators from Western colonialism. But it soon became clear that they were only interested in obtaining raw materials and treated military and civilians alike with contempt and frequent cruelty.

By now, the Americans were ready to fight back. In April 1942, sixteen B-25s flew over Tokyo, damaging sections of the city. In June, the Imperial Japanese Navy attempted to capture Midway Atoll, an American base in the Pacific. American planes taking off from three heavy-aircraft carriers intercepted the Japanese air attack and decisively defeated it, sinking four Japanese aircraft carriers. It was the beginning of the end for Japan.

For people at home, life was becoming intolerable. Even before Pearl Harbor, rice, vegetables, fish, and clothing had been rationed. People used to hot baths, good food, entertainment, and efficient public transport now faced hardship and deprivation.

In summer 1944, Saipan fell, followed by a succession of Pacific islands as American troops advanced on Japan. Tokyo was now within range of the B-29s.

Tōjō tried to conceal the disastrous state of the war from the Japanese public, but it was all too obvious. Behind closed doors, the business community, bureaucrats, and many politicians, notably the Anglophile ex-diplomat Yoshida Shigeru, had been counseling Konoe to surrender, and in July 1944, they managed to oust Tōjō. He was replaced by the equally implacable Koiso Kuniaki, who decided to strike back hard against the Americans.

As a last, desperate measure, military planners sent out forces of suicide bombers, *kamikaze*, named after the divine wind that drove off Kublai Khan's attempted invasion of Japan nearly seven hundred years earlier. Many were students who had been among the last to be conscripted. There were no return trips, which saved on precious fuel.

From January 1945, B-29s filled the skies, raining down firebombs on the cities. On one day, March 9, more than a hundred thousand people in Tokyo burned to death. Toward the end of May, there was a final blitz. The city was a wasteland of ash and rubble.

In July, the Allied leaders issued the Potsdam Declaration, demanding that Japan surrender unconditionally or face "prompt and utter destruction." Secret negotiations had been going on for some time. The stumbling block was the future position of the emperor.

The end came after the cities of Hiroshima and Nagasaki had been obliterated by atomic bombs. Some eighty thousand people were killed instantly in Hiroshima and fifty thousand in Nagasaki. Tens of thousands more later died of radiation sickness. At the same moment, the Soviet Army was sweeping into Manchuria. On August 15, people gathered around their radios to hear the emperor's reedy voice crackling over the airwaves. His people, he said, would have to "endure the unendurable and suffer the insufferable."

OCCUPATION

On August 30, 1945, the Supreme Commander for the Allied Powers, General Douglas MacArthur, stepped out of his plane onto the tarmac at Atsugi airfield. He was six feet tall, in uniform, with dark glasses, holding his corncob pipe in his hand. It was a supreme moment of theater. And it marked the beginning of an entirely new era for Japan.

The country MacArthur found himself in was utterly devastated. Few buildings still stood. The survivors were living in makeshift hovels. People stumbled around like ghosts.

Ensconced in his headquarters overlooking the ruins of the Imperial Palace, the "blue-eyed shogun" set about his task, to "reshape the Japanese mind," to turn Japan into a democracy that would never again go to war, following the directive drawn up by the State-War-Navy Coordinating Committee in Washington, DC.

The problem was that MacArthur and his fellow officers had only a limited understanding of Japan, the Japanese language, and the complexities of its political and business structures. Washington had ruled that they should work through Japanese bureaucrats and moderate political leaders, but it was difficult to be sure that these men were fully implementing their policies. Many were the very same people who had run the government during the war.

The first task was to demilitarize. The occupation officials dismantled the army and the navy and gave the territories that had formed the Japanese empire—Taiwan, Southeast Asia, a sizable part of China, and the other countries of the Greater East Asia Co-Prosperity Sphere—varying degrees of autonomy. They partitioned Korea, giving the south to the United States and the north to the Soviet Union.

This famous photograph shows MacArthur and Hirohito side by side, the tall American in his khaki uniform looming over the small, stiff emperor in his morning coat. The Americans published the picture widely to make it clear who was now in charge.

A week after MacArthur arrived, he had thirty-nine leading members of the government and military arrested and incarcerated in Sugamo prison. The question was what to do about the emperor. Should Hirohito be tried, or had he been an innocent bystander with no option but to rubber-stamp the decisions of the military? For most people, Hirohito still inspired devotion and to execute him might lead to open rebellion.

In the end, MacArthur decided to retain him as a symbol of the continuity and cohesion of the Japanese people. "Razor"

Tōjō would take the blame instead. The arrested men swore to protect the emperor from any hint of responsibility for the war and the occupation officials excluded any evidence that might incriminate members of the imperial family in the trials that followed.

Tōjō was hanged along with six others. Prince Asaka, who had overseen the massacre at Nanking, did not face trial. Konoe took cyanide before he could be arrested.

On January 1, 1946, at MacArthur's request, the emperor issued an imperial rescript denying his own divinity in terms that satisfied the Americans, though the Japanese interpretation was more ambivalent.

The following month, in just six days, the Americans drew up a constitution in which Japan renounced for all time the right to wage war. They abolished the peerage, pruned the imperial family, and pledged to dissolve the *zaibatsu*, the giant family conglomerates, which were held to have funded and supported the growth of militarism. Tens of thousands of people—members of ultranationalist groups, governors of former Japanese colonies, business leaders involved in overseas Japanese economic expansion, politicians, police, teachers—were purged from public service.

The constitution established a parliamentary system of government, gave women the vote, and guaranteed basic human rights, including the right to form unions. There was a major land reform. Overnight, five million tenants became owner-farmers, helping to create a wider domestic market and boosting industrial growth.

MacArthur encouraged everything that might further the democratic spirit—revolutionary gatherings, fiery speeches, calls for strikes. In October 1945, there was an amnesty for all those who had opposed the war. Suddenly everyone was talking about democracy, socialism, capitalism, and how society should develop. Young people marched, chanted, and devoured every issue of *Red Flag*.

That December, thousands gathered for the first postwar rally of the Communist Party. Shiga Yoshio, recently released after eighteen years in prison, addressed the crowd, who cheered when he denounced the emperor and added his name to the long list of war criminals.

The following month, Nosaka Sanzō returned after fifteen years in exile. A Japanese Che Guevara, idolized by left-wing intellectuals, he had cofounded the Japanese Communist Party and spent the war years in China, encouraging captured Japanese soldiers to fight for the Chinese communists against the Japanese Army. Under his guidance, the party pursued a policy of "lovable communism" and in the first postwar elections, in April 1946, won five seats in the diet.

Living conditions, meanwhile, were terrible. People died of starvation, exposure, pneumonia, typhus, cholera, and smallpox, or fought their way onto overcrowded trains to bring rice back to the cities. Women sold their kimonos layer by layer. Rations were meager, prices shot up, and wages were pitifully low. In May, the distribution system seized up and no rice arrived for three weeks. Led by Nosaka Sanzō, half a million people massed outside the Imperial Palace, demanding to know what the emperor had to eat.

Little by little, rebuilding got underway. By the end of 1948, the blueprint for the new Japan was largely in place. But there were many on both the American and Japanese sides who thought they'd gone too far.

REVERSE COURSE

After the first postwar elections, Yoshida Shigeru became prime minister. An urbane Anglophile who smoked cigars, wore pince-nez, and had a Churchillian square-jowled bulldog face, he had been ambassador to Britain for a couple of years. He was the person most responsible for laying the foundations of the new Japan.

Yoshida disagreed with many of the occupation's directives, such as renouncing war, making the emperor a constitutional monarch, breaking up the *zaibatsu*, and giving more rights to workers. He bided his time. He knew the occupation would end and a strong Japan would reemerge.

As he foresaw, events in the world at large soon forced America to rethink its plans for Japan. The turning point was 1949. America's relations with the Soviet Union had soured. The new bogey was world communism. The Americans did an about-face and embarked on what they called the Reverse Course. The aim now was to rebuild and rearm Japan, to make it a "Bulwark against Communism" and America's chief ally in Asia.

What saved Japan was the outbreak of the Korean War. Yoshida described it as "a gift from the gods." Mao Zedong's Communists had defeated Chiang Kai-shek's Kuomintang and established the People's Republic in neighboring China, then in 1950 intervened in the Korean War, threatening America's foothold in Japan.

Yoshida was now in a position to reverse some of the occupation's reforms. He de-purged thousands of conservatives and right-wing nationalists, who reentered politics and government ministries, and put plans to dissolve the *zaibatsu* on hold, then instituted a "red purge," removing Communist

Party members and sympathizers from the civil service, industry, and media and banning meetings and demonstrations in Tokyo. The Communist leader, Nosaka Sanzō, went into hiding.

With American troops leaving to fight in Korea, the United States wanted Japan to rearm. Yoshida established a police force, effectively an army, which became known as the Self-Defense Force. Japanese factories worked overtime to produce highly profitable munitions for the United Nations forces in Korea. By the time the war ended, Japan no longer needed direct American aid.

In 1951, Yoshida negotiated the San Francisco Treaty and a parallel defense treaty to restore Japanese sovereignty. Japan would receive preferential economic treatment and continue providing bases for US troops, aircraft, and ships and the United States would be responsible for its defense. When the treaties were ratified, Japan regained its independence amid general rejoicing.

The left, however, strongly opposed the treaties, which effectively made Japan a satellite of the United States. With no American troops to police the streets, there were riots, marches, strikes, and demonstrations against the government and the American bases firmly lodged on Japanese soil.

In the 1955 elections, the socialists won nearly half the votes. With the CIA pulling strings behind the scenes, the two main conservative parties joined forces to form the Liberal Democratic Party (LDP), the intention being to keep the left out of power forever.

Japan was well on the way to becoming the lively, prosperous place it had been before the war. With the help of American investment, industrial production doubled, tripled, then quadrupled. MacArthur's land reforms and the development of trade unions enabled more and more people to enjoy the benefits. Everyone wanted the "three treasures": television, washing machine, and refrigerator.

In 1957, Kishi Nobosuke became prime minister with CIA support. When he visited the United States, *Newsweek* called him the "friendly Savvy Salesman for Japan" who had created the "economic powerhouse of Asia."

Kishi was far from the friendly fellow that the Americans thought he was. A weak-chinned, weasel-faced Chōshū man, he had been the "economic king" of Manchukuo, using yakuza thugs to keep Chinese workers in line, and cosigned the declaration of war against the United States. After the war, he spent three years in prison but was de-purged because the Americans thought him the best man to head a right-leaning government that would do their bidding.

In 1959, he decided to revise the very unpopular US-Japan Security Treaty to give him the necessary heft to stay on for an unconstitutional third term. After signing the treaty, he invited President Dwight D. Eisenhower to visit Japan. But many Japanese hated the continuing presence of American troops on Japanese soil and thought the security treaty would drag Japan into another war.

Huge demonstrations filled the streets of Tokyo. More than six million workers went on strike and a million people besieged the National Diet building. In the end, Kishi withdrew Eisenhower's invitation four days before the visit was due. The treaty went through, but Kishi had to resign.

In encouraging Marxism, socialism, protest, and unions to flourish, MacArthur had let the genie out of the bottle. The question was how to get it back in again.

Yakuza

In 1959, when Prime Minister Kishi invited President Eisenhower to visit Japan, he called on Kodama Yoshio, his old friend from prison days, to provide thirty thousand yakuza to control protesters. Kodama, a shadowy godfather figure, linked the ultranationalists, the yakuza, and the right wing and was one of the most powerful men in Japan, eternally operating from behind the scenes.

Unlike their American counterparts, the Mafia, the yakuza were highly visible. Each yakuza "family" emblazoned their crest and family name on the wall of their headquarters. The yakuza wore badges indicating their affiliation and handed around business cards with their affiliation and rank, like Japanese businessmen. They strutted around in loud suits and careered through the narrow streets in huge American cars.

Each family was organized in a hierarchy with the boss at the top, to whom the lower ranks owed unswerving loyalty and obedience. If a yakuza committed an offense, he had to cut off the top joint of his left little finger in penance. Yakuza were famous for their spectacular whole-body tattoos depicting blossoms, dragons, or kabuki heroes in the style of woodblock prints.

Yakuza originated once peace was established in the 1600s, and began as peddlers and gamblers. The word yakuza ("good for nothing") is the worst possible combination of cards in a sort of blackjack: *ya* (8), *ku* (9), *za* (3). Their heyday was after World War II, when they controlled the black markets and played a big role in fighting leftists and trade unions during the occupation's clampdown on communism. At their peak in the early 1960s, there were more than two hundred thousand yakuza.

Today there are some twenty-five thousand. The yakuza inhabit the same neighborhoods as the red-light districts and the geisha, of whom there are several thousand, and are part of the same milieu. They run brothels, girly bars, pachinko parlors, gambling dens, and nightclubs, carry out extortion rackets, and smuggle drugs. They spread their tentacles over a huge range of industries—restaurants, bars, trucking companies—and have a cozy relationship with the police, who use them to put down demonstrations. They lend their threatening presence to business meetings and, through the likes of Kodama, wield power right to the top of government. Many politicians have yakuza links.

PUTTING THE GENIE BACK IN THE BOTTLE

On October 10, 1964, Sakai Yoshinori sprinted up 179 steps carrying the Olympic torch to set the enormous cauldron alight and signal the opening of the Tokyo Games. The 1964 Olympics marked the end of postwar hardship and poverty. This was the moment when Japan stepped onto the world stage to show off all that had been achieved.

Planning had begun from the moment the Games were awarded to Japan. In Tokyo, building went on night and day. In Harajuku, where the Games were to be held, the soaring curves of Tange Kenzō's spectacular Olympic stadium took shape. Boulevards were laid out to take Olympic traffic from the airport to the stadium. The showpiece was the *shinkansen* or "bullet train." The smoothest, fastest train in the world, linking Tokyo and Osaka at 135 miles (220 km) per hour, with streamlined carriages, a bullet-shaped nose, and luxurious seating, it opened in time for the Olympics.

For Japanese across the nation, it was a thrilling time. Emperor Hirohito, a small man in a black suit,

Sakai Yoshinori, the "Atomic Boy," was born in Hiroshima on the day the bomb fell.

described as the "patron," not the head of state, opened the Games. Japan took sixteen gold medals and placed third in the world stakes. The only disappointment was when a Dutchman won the all-important open-weight gold medal in judo, a sport which Japanese considered their own.

The person who finally put the genie back in the bottle was Kishi's successor. The soft-spoken, bespectacled Ikeda Hayato, the protégé of Yoshida Shigeru, realized that the best way to curb political dissent wasn't confrontation but conciliation. Put people to work, give them spending power, and they wouldn't bother with protest anymore. He made the seemingly impossible pledge to double the national income within ten years.

With Ikeda at the helm, Japanese businesses focused on efficiency and quality, using economies of scale to keep prices down. Japan was becoming the world's largest manufacturer of ships, cameras, televisions, cars, and synthetic fibers. Sony, Toshiba, Toyota, Honda, Panasonic, and Nissan became household names worldwide.

Almost immediately, it was obvious that Ikeda's policies were working. Standards of living shot up and material aspirations replaced the old political ideals.

Not everyone shared in the affluence or saw it as the solution to society's ills. The economic miracle had been achieved at the expense of living standards. Scandals forced the government to issue laws regulating pollution and compel offending companies to pay compensation. There was an underlying malaise. Was this all life was about—making money? Were the Japanese just "economic animals," men in suits, endlessly working?

In 1968 and 1969, there were huge uprisings against America's use of Japan as a staging base for its war in Vietnam and against the right-wing government. The protests became battles, with students fighting the police with staves, and forced the closure of campuses nationwide. When the US-Japan Security Treaty came up for renewal, there were more protests.

The celebrated novelist Mishima Yukio offered a bizarre response, hitting the headlines with a sensational protest, not of the left but of the right. In November 1970, he stepped onto the balcony of the headquarters of the Japan Ground Self-Defense Force. The army must rise up, he shouted, and restore the emperor to power. The soldiers, well-fed young men born long after the war, heckled and jeered. Mishima stepped inside, drew an antique sword, and cut open his belly in a formal *seppuku*.

Others expressed their rejection of the material- ism of Japanese society in their art and writing. This was the heyday of world-renowned directors such as Kurosawa Akira, whose films, such as *Seven Samurai* and *Yōjimbō*, introduced Western audi- ences to the dilemmas and heroism of the samurai era or, such as *Ikiru*, offered oblique commentary on the occupation and the years that followed it.

Mishima Yukio addressing the soldiers: Their response was sharp evidence of how much Japan had changed since its militaristic days.

There was a flourishing counterculture, many of whose boldest practitioners came from the neglected north. The dancer, choreographer, and wild man Hijikata Tatsumi devel- oped Butoh, a mesmeric performance art in which dancers with white-painted limbs and faces pushed their bodies to extremes. Terayama Shūji founded the avant-garde theater troupe Tenjō Sajiki, which performed iconoclastic, sometimes outrageous street theater.

In 1972, a new prime minister came to power. A north- erner with very little formal education, Tanaka Kakuei was a self-made man and a rabble-rouser, perpetually wiping sweat from his round, shiny face. With his wooden *geta* clogs and down-home personality, he was a breath of fresh air, and the most popular prime minister the country had seen for years. Three months after his election, he set out for China, following the lead of President Richard Nixon. He exerted his famous earthy charm on Mao Zedong and was able to restore diplomatic relations and sign a trade deal. He proclaimed 1973 the First Year of Welfare, doubling pensions and instituting free health care for the elderly and a universal child allowance.

But then, in October 1973, the Organization of Petroleum Exporting Countries (OPEC) declared an oil embargo. Six months later, the price of oil had tripled. It was a brutal end to the euphoria. The boom years had been fueled by cheap oil. Now there were long queues at gas stations. Ginza's neon lights, which had symbolized the economic miracle, dimmed and businesses went bankrupt.

Tanaka's popularity plummeted. Then *Bungei Shunjū*, a respected monthly, revealed the results of a lengthy probe into his complicated financial dealings. A good percentage of the funds earmarked for rural projects had ended up in his own pocket.

Worse was to come. Hauled up before a US Senate sub-committee, representatives of Lockheed Corporation confessed that while Tanaka was prime minister, they had funneled 1.8 million US dollars (16 million dollars in today's money) his way to ensure that All Nippon Airways purchased Lockheed aircraft. The yakuza kingpin Kodama Yoshio had overseen delivery of boxes crammed with cash.

Tanaka was arrested. But none of this affected the "shadow shogun's" grip on power. He continued to sit in the diet while on bail and gave his backing to Nakasone Yasuhiro, who became prime minister.

Then, in 1985, Tanaka had a severe stroke. He had dominated the political scene for more than ten years.

THE "BUBBLE YEARS"

August 15, 1985, was the fortieth anniversary of Japan's surrender at the end of World War II. At noon all over the country, bells tolled and people stood silent.

That day, defying large swaths of national and international opinion, Prime Minister Nakasone arrived at Yasukuni Shrine in a formal morning coat. He prayed for peace and for the souls of the war dead, offered flowers, and entered the inner sanctum, all highly symbolic acts.

Before World War II, Yasukuni had been the second-most revered shrine in State Shinto, the first being the grand shrine at Ise, which houses the Sun Goddess, Amaterasu. It was founded in 1869 to honor the souls of those who died fighting for the emperor and is dedicated to Japan's two and half million war dead. But these include General Tōjō Hideki and thirteen other Class A war criminals.

Nakasone was the first Japanese leader to make an official visit. It was a bold move, designed to placate the Japanese right wing. But many people were outraged, and the visit also angered the Chinese and South Koreans.

Nakasone had the knack of the grand gesture, although, as in his visit to Yasukuni, it didn't always work out. He was a gentleman, cool and aristocratic, the exact antithesis of Tanaka. Tall and statesmanlike, he was on "Ron-Yasu" terms with President Ronald Reagan. In photo sessions at summit meetings, instead of being hustled ignominiously to the end of the line like previous Japanese prime ministers, he stood in the middle, next to Reagan.

Under his leadership, Japan became a major player on the world stage. Even in the delicate matter of trade, he created a good relationship with the United States and consolidated the foundations Tanaka had laid in China.

Nakasone was on "Ron-Yasu" terms with President Reagan.

By the mid-1980s, Japan was very different from even a decade earlier. In Tokyo, the pace of change was frantic. The jerrybuilt blocks that had been thrown up after the war were replaced by buildings designed by the world's top architects. Wages were high, unemployment low, and there was excellent health care.

As Japan grew more and more prosperous, lifestyles were beginning to change. An earlier generation had assumed that their lives would revolve around their jobs. Their children demanded more leisure. Women who had been expected to stay home and oversee the household now demanded the option of working.

More and more people were migrating to the cities and living in nuclear families. In the past, families had taken care of their elderly, but now people wondered what would become of them. With fewer births and people living longer and longer, the population was aging at an alarming rate.

Japan focused on manufacturing and exporting cars and information technology, with such success that exports far outweighed imports. The dollar had risen very high, making it difficult for American manufacturers to compete with their Japanese rivals, whose goods were much cheaper in dollar terms. There were complaints that Japanese companies were undercutting their American competitors. In the United States, Japan-bashing became endemic. Republican senators smashed a Toshiba radio with sledgehammers on the Capitol lawn.

In September 1985, finance ministers from France, West Germany, Japan, the United Kingdom, and the United States met at the Plaza Hotel in New York to negotiate the Plaza Accord. The idea was to depreciate the dollar against the franc, mark, pound, and yen. The yen was allowed to float freely against the dollar.

In Japan, the effect was staggering. Overnight, the dollar tumbled and the price of imported goods practically halved. In dollar terms, everyone was twice as rich as they had been the day before.

Luxury cars became commonplace. People wore Chanel suits to go shopping. Students in trainers queued to buy necklaces at the Tiffany's outlet in Mitsukoshi department store.

For years, the Japanese had been a nation of savers. Now their children were learning to spend. According to the new ethic, if it was not expensive, it was not worth buying. People ate sushi scattered with gold flakes, indulged in a gold massage, or enjoyed the famous "two-hundred-dollar cup of coffee" just for the thrill of it. Japanese companies paid unprecedented prices for art. Yasuda Fire and Marine Insurance Company bought a Van Gogh *Sunflowers* for 39.9 million US dollars, more than twice the asking price. In 1987, the year that Nakasone's term of office came to an end, *Forbes* found more dollar billionaires in Japan than in the United States.

At the end of 1988, Japan fell silent. Hirohito was dying at the age of eighty-seven. Cabinet ministers excused themselves from international meetings, TV stations grew somber, corporations and schools canceled festivities.

The emperor died on January 7, 1989. World leaders attended the state funeral. A quarter of a million people lined the streets, sheltering under umbrellas, as the motorcade carried the coffin from the imperial palace to Shinjuku Gyoen Park, where the main rites were conducted. The coffin was transferred to a huge palanquin draped in gold with a black roof, carried by imperial court attendants who advanced at a funereal pace while otherworldly *gagaku* court music hung in the air.

Of the heads of state of the countries that had fought the Pacific War, Hirohito was the last to survive. The sixty-four years of his reign had seen Japan's fortunes plummet to their lowest and soar to the very highest. His death really did mark the end of an era.

CHAPTER 12

Heisei: Darker Years
1989–2019

In the Heisei ("Achieving Peace") era, the reign of Emperor Akihito, the great prosperity wave of the Shōwa era crested and crashed. It was an altogether darker time, marked by economic recession and calamities culminating in the tsunami and nuclear meltdown in Fukushima. Skyscrapers continued to spring up in Tokyo, but there were also growing numbers of homeless. After the euphoria of the 1980s, it was a reality check.

THE LOST DECADE

In August 1957, an earnest young man was playing tennis in the fashionable resort of Karuizawa when he was matched against a girl of startlingly radiant beauty. Shōda Michiko was the daughter of a wealthy industrialist but a commoner nonetheless and a Catholic. Until then, it would have been impossible for a crown prince to even think of marrying anyone but an imperial princess.

But these were different times. Emperor Akihito had been tutored by a Quaker, Elizabeth Gray Vining, appointed by the occupation forces to teach him English, democracy, and Christianity. His fairy-tale romance with Michiko galvanized the nation.

After Akihito came to the throne, he demonstrated how different his reign was going to be by visiting China; he was the first emperor ever to do so. He didn't go so far as to apologize for Japan's wartime aggression but acknowledged that his country had "inflicted severe suffering upon the Chinese people" and added, "This is a deep sorrow to me."

The year of his accession, 1989, was a time of seismic change for the world. The Berlin Wall fell, uniting East and West Germany; President George H. W. Bush and Mikhail Gorbachev, leader of the Soviet Union, declared the Cold War officially over; and the Soviet Union started to break up.

Meanwhile, Japan continued to surf the wave of prosperity. The so-called "Heisei aristocrats" were wealthy thanks to soaring land and stock prices and to Japanese banks, which handed out billions of yen in loans at very low interest rates. In 1989, Sony took over Columbia Pictures, while Mitsubishi bought a controlling stake in Rockefeller Center, sparking outrage among Americans, who complained that Japan was buying up the world.

That turned out to be the crest of the wave. The following year, the Ministry of Finance raised interest rates, aiming to bring down the soaring prices. The ploy misfired. Stock and land prices tumbled and the great Japanese economic bubble burst. Bankruptcies and unemployment soared, and employers clamped down on overtime. Suddenly it was possible to find an empty taxi late at night or get a table at a French restaurant without booking ahead. Diamonds were left on the shelf, the sales of Mercedes slackened, and instead of designer labels, the fashion was for jeans. The collapse continued over the so-called Lost Decade.

The Liberal Democratic Party (LDP) still monopolized power, but after Nakasone's glory years, a succession of prime ministers were brought low by corruption scandals and incompetence. One lasted just sixty-eight days and was felled by his geisha ex-mistress, who accused him of being tight-fisted, the ultimate shame.

Eventually, in 1993, the LDP was voted out of power for the first time in thirty-eight years. A coalition of opposition parties took over, and for a while it looked as if there might be real change. But after less than a year, the LDP was back in control.

The economy continued to plummet. But for all the doom-laden statistics, Japan remained a country with a very low crime rate where most people were well fed and well dressed. Many people had become wealthy enough during the bubble years to avoid the worst of the collapse. For some, the fall in land prices meant that they could now afford to buy a house. The parties continued, the cities were as glamorous as ever, and glossy new skyscrapers continued to mushroom. As one British diplomat remarked, "If this is a recession, I'd like one."

But there were growing numbers of casualties. As men found themselves out of work and hanging around the house, women started suing for divorce. Men who couldn't repay their debts or bear the shame of unemployment committed suicide. Some put on a business suit every morning and then hid in a park so that no one would know they had no job. Encampments of homeless living in cardboard boxes, with their shoes and umbrellas outside, sprang up in parks and around railway stations. Many were from the much poorer north and had come to Tokyo to look for work in vain.

Then one January morning in 1995, a mammoth earthquake, 7.2 on the Richter scale, jolted the city of Kobe. Four hundred thousand buildings collapsed and nearly 6,500 people died. Road and rail bridges fell, pipelines broke, fires raged across the city, and a huge elevated expressway crashed down. Long before the official emergency response began, the yakuza, in Robin Hood mode, moved in, setting up soup kitchens and distributing supplies. The government was shamefully unprepared. There were no relief centers, the response was way too slow, and they actively prevented Japanese and American troops from stepping in to help. In a display of people power, volunteers from all over Japan converged on the stricken city.

In this land of volcanoes, hot springs, and regular tremors, earthquakes, while devastating, were not unexpected. But what happened next was a total shock. That March, five men boarded subway trains carrying plastic bags of liquid sarin at the peak of the morning rush hour. Twelve people died and thousands were horribly injured from inhaling the deadly gas.

The attacks were the work of a doomsday cult called Aum Shinrikyō, led by the bearded, charismatic Asahara Shōkō. Thirteen of the leaders were executed, including Asahara, and many more went to prison.

The episode sparked much soul-searching about what had happened to Japan to inspire such alienation. Writers such as Murakami Haruki saw it as a manifestation of existential crisis; people had lost their core values and beliefs and been left lacking direction, meaning, or purpose.

It pointed up the fragmentation of Japanese society, brought about by the long recession. Where once, in theory at least, Japan had been monolithic, a nation of salarymen working away at lifetime employment, now, for many, lifetime employment was no longer an option and more and more people were choosing to carve out their own paths. Nonconformity had become a lifestyle choice.

Disaffection took many forms. There were *freeters*, freelancers who moved from job to job, and *neets*, "not in education, employment, or training." Teenagers formed tribes, adopting outrageous costumes, hairstyles, and hair colors. Girls dressed like cartoon characters, while leather-clad teddy boys with oiled upswept hair danced to rock 'n' roll in Tokyo's Yoyogi Park.

Otaku, "nerds," characteristically unwashed and scruffy, pursued their chosen obsession—manga, anime, video games, cars, pop idols—flouting the Japanese norm of fitting in. Most extreme of all were *hikikomori*, who locked themselves in their bedrooms, usually in their parents' homes, sometimes for years on end.

Then, in April 2001, a prime minister appeared who seemed infinitely more attuned to this new, fragmented, non-consensus Japan.

JAPAN REJOINS THE WORLD

When President George W. Bush took Koizumi Junichirō to Graceland, the Japanese prime minister warbled a rendition of "Love Me Tender" and showed off a few Elvis moves. Bush, grinning broadly, commented, "This visit here shows that not only am I personally fond of the prime minister, but the ties between our peoples are very strong as well."

Koizumi was a master of image. With his long, wavy hair and casual clothes, he was radically different from his stodgy, besuited predecessors. He was known for his direct style, idiosyncratic approach, and refusal to go along with LDP consensus politics. He framed himself as a maverick standing up against the stuffy Japanese elite on behalf of the people.

As the economy recovered, his popularity surged. He bailed out Japan's banks, cut back on public spending, and deregulated the labor markets, encouraging companies to take on short-term contract workers.

Koizumi Junichirō shows off his Elvis moves to George W. Bush at Graceland while Priscilla Presley and Lisa Marie Presley look on.

In 2004, Bush asked Koizumi to send troops to help with the occupation and reconstruction of Iraq after the United States–led invasion. It was the first time that Japanese troops had operated abroad other than as part of a United Nations mission. This escalation in military activity breached the peace constitution and was hugely controversial. Worse, Koizumi was supporting the United States, which had invaded Iraq without United Nations sanction.

Koizumi was no liberal. Throughout his six years as prime minister, he made the annual pilgrimage to Yasukuni Shrine, arguing that he was fulfilling a campaign promise. In response, China and South Korea refused to send representatives to Japan. There were anti-Japanese riots in China and anger at home.

Emperor Akihito chose this moment to speak up, stating that he felt "a certain kinship with Korea" as, according to the *Nihon Shoki* (*Chronicles of Japan*), the mother of his ancestor, the great Emperor Kanmu, had come from the Korean kingdom of Baekje, and expressing gratitude that Koreans had brought Buddhism, Confucianism, and court music to Japan from China. It was the first time anyone, let alone the emperor, had dared mention that the imperial family might have Korean roots, and Akihito's words made headlines. There was even a suggestion that he might visit Korea, though in the end the plan fell through.

The flamboyant Koizumi was succeeded by a succession of mainly forgettable prime ministers who lasted little more than a year each. The only memorable one was Abe Shinzō, who resigned because of ill health and who was to become prime minister again in 2012 for a record-breaking three terms.

Eventually, the Democratic Party of Japan (DPJ) won a landslide victory, making their leader, Hatoyama Yukio, prime minister. He was young, appealing, and eager to build stronger links with Asia, and there were high hopes for real change. But he, too, was brought down by a corruption scandal and resigned in June 2010.

Then came an event that put everything into perspective, challenging not just Japan's beleaguered political system but everyone's conceptions of what life was all about.

THE GREAT WAVE

At 2:46 in the afternoon of March 11, 2011, there was a rumble like thunder as the earth began to move. The violent shaking went on for an excruciating six minutes as people dived for shelter or clung to whatever they could find. Buildings crumpled, roads and railways cracked, and fires burst out. The epicenter was off the coast of Fukushima in Tōhoku, the impoverished northeast.

The quake was more intense and continued for longer than anyone had ever experienced before. It was 9.1 on the Richter scale, the most powerful earthquake ever recorded in Japan and the fourth most powerful in the world since records began. It shifted the Earth on its axis and moved Honshu island 8 feet (2.5 m) to the east.

Half an hour later, a wall of gray water some 130 feet (40 m) high, the height of a twelve-story building, came roaring across the ocean at 435 miles per hour (700 km/h), toppling seawalls like matchwood. As sirens wailed, people fled to evacuation areas or jumped into their cars and accelerated toward high ground.

The tsunami surged in, smashing everything in its path, scooping up boats, cars, people, buildings, bridges, and houses and carrying them inland, then slamming them down or sucking them back out to sea. Whole towns were wiped off the map. People running back to look for survivors were swept up by further tsunamis that came roaring in.

Nearly twenty thousand people were killed or never found, including several hundred schoolchildren. Thousands were injured and hundreds of thousands made homeless.

Along the coast, eleven reactors at the four Fukushima nuclear power plants shut down automatically when the earthquake hit. The tsunami, however, disabled the backup generators needed to pump water into the reactors to cool the nuclear fuel when the plant was off. The pumps stopped, the water level in the cores began to fall, and the reactors started to boil. Steam built up and a mammoth hydrogen explosion tore through reactor number 1, blasting out a cloud of radioactive smoke. The fuel continued to burn, releasing more radiation.

Tokyo Electric Power Company (TEPCO) declared an emergency and the government ordered 164,000 people living in a twelve-mile zone around the plant to evacuate immediately. People found themselves crowded into evacuation centers with little food, heat, or water, dependent on donations for hot meals and warm clothing.

In the following weeks the cleanup and rebuilding began, though with huge difficulty. But no one knew what the effect of the radiation would be, how far it would spread, or what effect it might have on agriculture.

Once again, politicians showed themselves inadequate to the task. The DPJ prime minister resigned, as did the next. In December 2012, the LDP joined forces with another center-right party, promising strong government. They won a landslide victory and Abe Shinzō became prime minister for the second time. The country heaved a collective sigh of relief. Finally, there was a strong hand on the tiller.

SUPER MARIO SAVES JAPAN

At the end of the closing ceremony for the 2016 Olympics in Rio de Janeiro, a familiar red-clad figure in blue overalls emerged from a green wormhole, having apparently traveled at warp speed straight through the earth from Tokyo. It was the buoyant Nintendo character Super Mario, resplendent in trademark cap and carrying a large red ball. He threw off his red-and-blue outfit to reveal himself as Prime Minister Abe, waved his cap in the air and, as the ball lit up in a blaze of light, invited the entire world to the next Games—in Tokyo.

Abe was the grandson of Kishi Nobosuke, the Class A war criminal who pushed through the US-Japan Security

Treaty, sparking huge riots. Nevertheless, Kishi had been a strong prime minister, and Abe's pedigree gave people confidence that he knew what he was doing.

Finally, there was something to work for. Just as the 1964 Olympics had been a chance for Japan to show how much had been achieved since the war, the 2020 Games would allow Japan to emerge from the shadow of Fukushima.

Abe's mission was to make Japan strong again. In a speech in Washington, DC, he announced, "Japan is back!" Economically, the country was in the doldrums. There had been very little growth for the last twenty years and

Abe Shinzō as Super Mario at the Rio Olympics: Like Koizumi, he had flair and showmanship.

problems had been exacerbated by the Fukushima disaster. He fired off an ambitious program, "Abenomics," to reboot the economy. Economic growth picked up, exports rose, and unemployment dropped to its lowest level in two decades.

Other areas of his policy platform were a lot less palatable. Building a strong Japan meant rewriting school textbooks to water down war crimes such as the Nanking massacre. He also declared in the face of claims from Korean "comfort women" that there was no evidence that the Japanese military had forced women into sexual slavery during World War II.

Most controversially, Abe was determined to revise the peace clause in Japan's constitution. In 2015, he sparked furious rows in the diet and huge demonstrations on the streets outside, reminiscent of the anti-Security Treaty demonstrations of his grandfather's day, when he pushed through legislation allowing Japan to exercise "collective self-defense," to come to the aid of an ally under attack; Japan could now come to America's defense as well as America defending Japan. His rationale was the growing threat from China and North Korea and wrangling over the Senkaku Islands, claimed by China, South Korea, and Taiwan as well as by Japan, combined with America's growing reluctance to become involved in regional issues on Japan's behalf.

He also clamped down on dissent at home. There were more demonstrations in 2017 when he pushed through anti-terrorism laws to limit public protest, criminalizing a wide variety of activities.

Abe was still riding the wave when the end of the era arrived without fanfare in 2019. Emperor Akihito had stated several years earlier that his health was failing. The government enacted a one-time law to enable him to abdicate, and on April 30, 2019, at the age of eighty-five, he did so.

Cool Japan

As was to be expected of a man who had worn the mantle of Super Mario, Abe appreciated the potency of Cool Japan. Japan didn't have to win wars. It could win by exporting culture.

From the 1980s onward, Japan was the embodiment of cool. Japan's exploding subculture set trends worldwide. Fads such as cosplay ("costume play," where participants, usually teenage girls, dress as anime, manga, and other fictional characters) and *otaku* (nerds or outsiders) permeated youth culture. Japanese manga and anime were world famous, starting with the legendary Tezuka Osamu's *Astro Boy* in the 1950s and Studio Ghibli's many marvelous films such as *My Neighbor Totoro*. There were video games such as Nintendo and characters such as Super Mario, Pokémon, and Tamagotchi, the digital pet. Japanese food was a cult in itself, as was Japanese fashion, from Issey Miyake's iconic pleats to Japan's wild and wacky street fashion.

In 2008, Cool Japan became official government policy and the blue, earless cat Doraemon was chosen as Japan's Anime Ambassador. He appeared at the 2016 Rio Olympics to promote Japan and again at the 2020 Tokyo Olympics.

CHAPTER 13

Reiwa: A New Emperor for a New Age
2019–Present

The early years of the Reiwa ("Beautiful Harmony") era were marked by the COVID-19 pandemic, upending plans for the 2020 Olympics, and by Russia's invasion of Ukraine, which exacerbated tensions in East Asia. In response, Japan decided it was high time to move away from the peace clause in its constitution and rejoin the world as a military power. It was a watershed moment.

A NEW ERA

The Reiwa era opened with the state visit of President Donald Trump, the first world leader to meet Emperor Naruhito, just weeks after his accession. Trump declared with characteristic bombast that this would be "the biggest event they [Japan] have had in two hundred years." His visit came at the personal invitation of Prime Minister Abe, who made it clear what a huge and historic honor it was.

At the Imperial Palace, Trump was greeted by Naruhito and Empress Masako with enormous pomp and pageantry. He reviewed the troops before being ushered into the palace for an elaborate state banquet. He also attended a sumo match and presented the winner with the massive President's Cup, topped with an eagle.

Naruhito and Masako were married on June 9, 1993.

Naruhito was a youthful fifty-nine when he succeeded his father. In many ways, he was the embodiment of the modern Japanese man. He spoke English, having studied at Oxford, and, far from having an arranged marriage, had a well-publicized love story. He met the love of his life and for six years tried fruitlessly to persuade her to accept him, inspiring ribald articles in the Japanese tabloids about why he was still single into his thirties.

Owada Masako was a diplomat's daughter and a career diplomat herself who had spent much of her early life in Russia and the United States. She finally agreed to marry Naruhito after he promised to take care of her "with all my power." Her reluctance to become crown princess proved well founded. Like her mother-in-law, Empress Michiko, she suffered bullying as a commoner inside the rigid ranks of the imperial household. At a formal dinner, she chatted with Bill Clinton in English and with Boris Yeltsin in Russian and was later reprimanded for upstaging the emperor. From having been a globe-trotting diplomat, she found herself confined to the palace, where her only duty was to produce an heir. It was a long and difficult nine years before Princess Aiko was born in 2001.

By the time Trump visited, all this was in the past. Abe, whose policy of making Japan strong seemed to match Trump's "Make America Great Again," had courted Trump from the moment he became president and Trump regarded him as a friend. Yet, unlike his predecessors, Trump saw Japan as an economic rival, not an ally, and wanted to increase trade tariffs. "I remember Pearl Harbor," he told Abe menacingly, if somewhat anachronistically. There was also the issue of North Korea, which had abducted Japanese citizens and fired sophisticated missiles disturbingly close to Japan. Trump had shown himself worryingly friendly to North Korea's erratic leader, Kim Jong-un.

Abe's mission was to shake off the shackles of the peace constitution, which he saw as outdated, but the opposition steadfastly voted against revision. For decades, Japan had faced few military threats. But now it was surrounded by hostile neighbors. As China grew wealthier and more powerful, it made strident claims to a cluster of minute, uninhabited islands in the South and East China Seas, the crucial feature being that there was oil there. China's defense budget was ten times that of Japan and it was beefing up its nuclear arsenal. Relations with South Korea were also bad because of the comfort women issue, while Russia laid claim to some small islands up north. And none of these neighbors had forgotten the brutal Japanese occupation.

Japan was hobbled by its pacifist constitution and had a tiny military relative to its economic strength. It badly needed the support of the American alliance.

Meanwhile, preparations went on apace for the 2020 Tokyo Olympics. The watchword was *omotenashi*, "hospitality," and Japanese businesses paid small fortunes to add the tag "Tokyo 2020" to their advertising.

The Games were far from uncontroversial. They were touted as the Recovery Olympics, to show the world that Japan had rebuilt after the Fukushima nuclear catastrophe. But as activists pointed out, money and effort were poured into the new national stadium while the Fukushima survivors were all but forgotten.

The stadium, to replace Tange Kenzō's iconic 1964 building, had been commissioned from Zaha Hadid, a celebrity architect. She designed a vast building that, as many people joked, looked like a gargantuan cycling helmet. Japanese architects complained that the government had commissioned a foreign architect instead of one of them and the projected cost spiraled to a breathtaking 252 billion yen (1.8 billion US dollars).

In 2015, Abe decided to cancel it. A new design was commissioned from a Japanese architect to reflect traditional Japanese architecture and be more in keeping with its surroundings and more ecologically friendly. It was constructed largely of local timber from Japan's forty-seven prefectures.

Preparations were nearly in place for the Games and the excitement was growing when something totally unexpected happened that brought the whole world to a halt.

OLYMPICS AT A TIME OF PLAGUE

The COVID-19 virus broke out in Wuhan, China, in December 2019 and on January 20, 2020, a traveler returning to Japan was found to be ill. This was a singularly dangerous disorder, a respiratory disease that spread like wildfire and caused a significant number of deaths.

As the gravity of the situation became apparent, worldwide shutdowns began in an effort to prevent the spread of the disease. Japanese habits made the nation better fitted to deal with the pandemic than many other countries: people wore masks as a matter of course when ill, bowed rather than shook hands or hugged, followed guidelines without resenting them, and kept everything spotless.

Abe closed schools and sports arenas and in April declared a state of emergency. First the cities, then the whole country was required to self-isolate. In reality, most people carried on going to work and to restaurants, and entertainment venues remained open. Sports events continued with the grounds half filled. Initially, the Japanese model seemed to work, with rates of infection and deaths by far the lowest among developed nations. Nevertheless, there were protests against the government's methods.

The most pressing issue was the Games, which were coming up fast. There were complaints that instead of focusing on the virus, the government was more concerned with saving the Games. Even Trump asked for them to be postponed.

Finally, Abe, in tandem with the International Olympic Committee (IOC), decided to postpone them for a year for the first time in their history. In August, he resigned due to a long-standing ailment. His eight-year term made him Japan's longest-serving prime minister. He handed what was in effect a poisoned chalice to an LDP stalwart, Suga Yoshihide.

As 2021 dawned, COVID still held the world in its deadly grip. The question was whether to hold the Games that year or to cancel them altogether. Japan's borders had been sealed for over a year. If the Olympics went ahead, fifteen thousand athletes would arrive, plus tens of thousands of officials, judges, media, and volunteers. Only 2 percent of the population was fully vaccinated. The country was in the throes of a fourth wave of infections, with many cities, including Tokyo, under a third state of emergency. The hospitals were overwhelmed. Protesters paraded with banners outside the new National Stadium, and doctors and nurses were particularly vocal.

The IOC, blatantly putting profits ahead of public health, announced that the Games would go ahead irrespective of public opinion and whether there was a state of emergency in Tokyo. Suga concurred. This was an election year, but the LDP was so firmly entrenched that even a disastrous Olympics would not affect his prospects.

In the end, the Olympics did take place. All the events were held behind closed doors. As Japanese athletes began to win medals, public opinion changed and the Games were judged a success, though predictably they triggered a massive wave of new COVID cases.

Suga's ratings had plummeted because of his failures over the coronavirus. He was replaced by Kishida Fumio, who was seen as a safe pair of hands and had been the foreign affairs minister for an unprecedented five years under Abe.

In July 2022, Abe himself was in Nara delivering a campaign speech for an LDP candidate when a young man stepped forward wielding a handmade gun and shot him dead. It was a brutal end to a momentous career and the most shocking of events, particularly in a peaceful country such as Japan, where guns were strictly prohibited.

The killer was arrested immediately. It transpired that he had been bankrupted by the Unification Church, a cult known as the Moonies, founded in 1954 by Sun Myung Moon, a South Korean religious leader. He was incensed because Abe and many other LDP politicians had links with the church right back to Kishi, Abe's grandfather, because of its anti-communist stance. Abe, too, had given speeches in support of it.

Abe's death entrenched the LDP even further. In the election two days later, a sympathy vote ensured that they won a huge majority in the upper house.

Abe had been a polarizing figure, revered by the right and hated by the left as he used his party's comfortable majority in the diet to undermine the peace clause in the constitution. He was given a state funeral, usually reserved for members of the imperial family. There were violent protests at the cost and at honoring such a controversial figure.

By 2022, the world seemed to have found a way to live with the coronavirus. Then, on February 24, the day after the emperor's birthday, war exploded in Europe.

INTO THE FUTURE

The LDP was still struggling to revise the peace constitution, the problem being that a majority of the public was vociferously against developing any kind of military capability. Then Russia invaded Ukraine. The invasion made a Chinese invasion of Taiwan, a mere 100 miles (160 km) from Japan's westernmost point, a distinct and frightening possibility.

That August, after House Speaker Nancy Pelosi visited Taipei, Beijing conducted military exercises, sending five missiles into Japanese waters. Meanwhile, North Korea threatened to turn the Pacific "into a firing range." In October, a particularly powerful ballistic missile flew across Japan, forcing people to evacuate. Other missiles followed.

In this more hostile environment, a chastened public would surely be more likely to support the beefing up of Japan's military. Kishida took as his watchword, "What happened in Ukraine may happen in East Asia tomorrow."

In December 2022, he put forward a radical new national security strategy that would allow Japan's armed forces to counterstrike in response to a perceived threat from China, North Korea, or Russia, rather than just maintaining a defensive posture. He announced a doubling of defense spending to 2 percent of GDP by 2027, equaling the NATO benchmark and making Japan's military budget the third largest in the world after the United States and China. He put in place plans to buy five hundred Tomahawk cruise missiles from the United States, powerful enough to put Chinese and North Korean military bases within striking distance, and to develop Japan's own weapons systems further, thus shouldering more of the burden of defense in the region.

These were steps none of his predecessors had dared to take. There was a mixed response at home, with political opponents declaring that Kishida was using his liberal image to put forward unacceptably aggressive policies.

In the months that followed, Kishida moved swiftly to establish Japan's place as a major player on the world stage, freed from its postwar peace constitution and functioning in every way as a normal country. In March 2023, he made an unannounced trip to Kyiv, making him the first Japanese leader to visit an active war zone in nearly half a century.

He also brought about rapprochement with South Korea for the first time since World War II. He invited South Korean president Yoon Suk Yeol to Tokyo in March, then went to Seoul himself in May, and spontaneously said that his "heart hurt" at the thought of the suffering that Koreans had endured during World War II, though he didn't go so far as to issue an official apology. The two leaders firmed up the détente at a meeting at Camp David that August, hosted by President Joe Biden.

Kishida made a point of focusing on relations with the Pacific and East Asia in response to the threat to Taiwan. In 2023, Japan took its turn as head of the Group of Seven (G7) world leaders and in May hosted a meeting of heads of state in Hiroshima, to which Kishida invited President Yoon, Prime Minister Narendra Modi of India, and other heads of non-G7 countries, aiming to further Japan's Free and Open Indo-Pacific agenda to counter China's influence in the region. Later that year, he met Chinese president Xi Jinping for trade talks, smoothing the economic relationship between the two countries despite their deep-seated political disagreements.

In April 2024, he was in Washington, DC, on a state visit—an honor reserved for America's closest allies. There, he enjoyed a grand state banquet attended by Hollywood stars, former presidents, and the superstar Japanese pop duo Yoasobi, who tamed their normally wild appearance for the occasion.

The two leaders announced a "new era" in their relationship, cementing the alliance between their countries and marking Japan's emergence as an equal partner with the US in the face of China's growing assertiveness in East Asia. But there was an unspoken agenda, too: to shore up the alliance against a possible return to power of former president Donald J. Trump, whose unpredictable foreign policy decisions have been worrying many in Japan.

Away from the political field, Japan successfully launched its small octagonal Smart Lander for Investigating Moon (SLIM, nicknamed Moon Sniper), which arrived on the moon within a few yards of its intended target in January 2024 after a four-month journey. Admittedly, it landed awkwardly in a crater and had difficulty getting its solar panels to work, but nevertheless it was cause for celebration, making Japan one of only five countries to make a soft landing on the lunar surface.

Japanese citizens also looked forward to the Osaka Expo, scheduled to open in April 2025 with the optimistic theme of "Designing Future Society for Our Lives."

There are several issues to consider as Japan heads into the future. The birthrate is falling steeply and the population is aging rapidly, resulting in fewer and fewer workers and a need for more caregivers for the elderly. Japan is at the forefront in developing robot caregivers, but they are still a work in progress. Immigrant workers are one solution to the problem of a dwindling workforce. As the government loosens controls on immigration, Japan is getting used to being more diverse. Foreign sumo wrestlers once suffered discrimination. Now some are celebrated *yokozuna*, grand champions.

Then there are Japan's outlying territories, taken over in the Meiji period. In Hokkaido, the Ainu, perhaps descendants of the Jōmon, were given recognition as an indigenous population of Japan in 2019, but they still endure discrimination and poor living conditions. Okinawa, once the independent kingdom of the Ryukyus, is dominated by American bases, a problem that will only increase as the dispute over the islands of the South China Sea grows more intense. There are also Japanese of Korean descent, who until recently were treated as second-class citizens.

The issue of comfort women, forced to work in wartime brothels for the Japanese military, has still not been fully resolved. It is estimated that up to 410,000 women, many of Korean descent, were forcibly removed for sexual slavery by imperial Japan. In a landmark deal in 2015, the Japanese government apologized and offered to provide 1 billion yen (8.5 million US dollars) in compensation. But the deal turned out to be flawed. It had been put together primarily to smooth out relations between Japan and Korea, and the women themselves had not been consulted. They demanded much more. Meanwhile, the remaining women are gradually dying. There are only a few left.

There is also the urgent issue of climate change, which in 2023 brought an unprecedented heat wave to Japan, as to much of the northern hemisphere. Japan has been shaped by natural disasters and the Japanese are uniquely prepared for earthquakes, typhoons, tsunamis, floods, and volcanic eruptions. Nevertheless, climate change presents new and unexpected hazards. Japan has committed to the United Nations climate change initiative to reduce greenhouse gases and it also supports developing countries affected by climate change.

Japan has long had a complicated relationship with the outside world. During the Edo period, the Tokugawa shoguns successfully closed the country to the West. After Japan opened up, it swung in the opposite direction, adopting Western culture wholesale, reshaping Japan on the Western model. Both these strategies enabled it to avoid colonization, one of the very few non-Western countries to do so, and to retain its unique cultural traditions and way of life. No matter how Western Japan might appear, it still feels different, due to its legacy as an island nation and to the long years of separate development.

The Japanese also have a complex relationship with their own past. Until recently, the Edo period was portrayed as backward and feudal in novels such as Shimazaki Tōson's *Before the Dawn*, the "dawn" being the Meiji Restoration. It was only in 1993, with the opening of the Edo-Tokyo Museum in Tokyo, that people started to consider Edo culture as something to be proud of. Today there is a huge amount of interest in Japan's own history, with Jōmon and Yayoi settlements being unearthed across the country. All this is tied to *nihonjinron*—the question of what it means to be Japanese.

Nevertheless, Japan remains an extraordinarily prosperous and successful society. Most people enjoy comfortable lives and the crime rate is enviably low. It's a well-ordered, efficient place where skyscrapers continue to mushroom and the bullet trains run strictly on time.

Japan has found a unique way of reconciling past and present, being a hugely successful modern nation while also nurturing its ancient traditions, customs, and culture. The emperor is perhaps Japan's most potent link with the past. He binds the nation together, perpetuating ancient rituals such as the Daijosai, the enthronement ceremony. While British royals join the military and cover their chests in medals, in Japan the proper calling for royalty is scholarship. Emperor Hirohito carried out research in marine biology and Akihito writes scientific papers on ichthyology. Naruhito studied at Oxford and wrote a thesis on the history of transportation on the Thames. He and the rest of the imperial family write and publish annual New Year's poems.

Japanese culture has not just endured but strengthened. People practice tea ceremony, flower arrangement, Zen, haiku, and martial arts, and the rebuilt kabuki theater, which reopened in 2013 in Tokyo, is as popular as ever. Westerners, too, enthusiastically study Japanese arts, from the impressionists collecting woodblock prints to architects inspired by the clean lines of Japanese traditional housing.

Amaterasu in a modern incarnation

Thus, Japan's extraordinary culture has survived the vicissitudes of the centuries. Yoshimitsu's Golden Pavilion gleams in Kyoto, despite having been burned down by a mad monk. Hōryūji, the world's oldest wooden building, still stands in Nara, and Tōdaiji still houses Emperor Shōmu's Great Buddha. Amaterasu's shrine at Ise is still rebuilt every twenty years and visitors arrive in their thousands to pay their respects and ask her protection. Amaterasu has also found new life in films and as a character in manga. Far from being a historical relic, she is as alive today as she was before time began.

Further Reading

Beasley, W. G., *The Meiji Restoration* (Stanford, CA: Stanford University Press, 1972).

——, *The Rise of Modern Japan* (Tokyo: Charles E. Tuttle Co., 1990).

Bix, Herbert P., *Hirohito and the Making of Modern Japan* (New York: HarperCollins, 2000).

Buruma, Ian, *A Japanese Mirror: Heroes and Villains of Japanese Culture* (London: Jonathan Cape, 1984).

Cortazzi, Hugh (ed.), *Mitford's Japan: Memories and Recollections 1866–1906* (London: Athlone Press, 1985).

Diamond, Jared, "In Search of Japanese Roots," *Discover Magazine*, June 1, 1998.

Dower, John, *Embracing Defeat: Japan in the Wake of World War II* (New York: W. W. Norton & Co., 1999).

Downer, Lesley, *On the Narrow Road to the Deep North: Journey into a Lost Japan* (London: Jonathan Cape, 1989).

——, *The Brothers: The Hidden World of Japan's Richest Family* (New York: Random House, 1994).

——, *Women of the Pleasure Quarters: The Secret History of the Geisha* (New York: Broadway Books, 2001).

Fletcher, Robert S. G., *The Ghost of Namamugi: Charles Lenox Richardson and the Anglo-Satsuma War* (Folkestone, UK: Renaissance Books, 2019).

Frydman, Joshua, *The Japanese Myths: A Guide to Gods, Heroes and Spirits* (London: Thames & Hudson, 2022).

Gluck, Carol, *Japan's Modern Myths: Ideology in the Late Meiji Period* (Princeton: Princeton University Press, 1985).

Gluck, Carol, *Showa: The Japan of Hirohito* (New York: W W Norton & Company Inc., 1990).

Gordon, Andrew, *A Modern History of Japan* (Oxford, UK: Oxford University Press, 2013).

Habu, Junko, *Ancient Jōmon of Japan* (Cambridge, UK: Cambridge University Press, 2012).

Harding, Christopher, *The Japanese: A History in Twenty Lives* (London: Allen Lane, 2020).

Hibbett, Howard, *The Floating World in Japanese Fiction* (Clarendon, VT: Tuttle Publishing, 2001).

Iyer, Pico, *A Beginner's Guide to Japan: Observations and Provocations* (New York: Bloomsbury Publishing, 2019).

Jansen, Marius, *The Making of Modern Japan* (Cambridge, MA: Harvard University Press, 2002).

Jansen, Marius (ed.), *The Cambridge History of Japan*, volumes 1–6 (Cambridge, UK: Cambridge University Press, 1989).

Kaempfer, Engelbert, *Kaempfer's Japan: Tokugawa Culture Observed*, trans. Beatrice M. Bodart Bailey (Honolulu: University of Hawai'i Press, 1999).

Kaner, Simon (ed.), *The Power of Dogu: Ceramic Figures from Ancient Japan* (London: British Museum Press, 2009).

Keene, Donald, (ed.), *Anthology of Japanese Literature: From the Earliest Era to the Mid-Nineteenth Century* (New York: Grove Press, 1955).

Kobayashi, Tatsuo, *Jōmon Reflections: Forager Life and Culture in the Prehistoric Japanese Archipelago* (Oxford, UK: Oxbow Books, 2004).

Lloyd Parry, Richard, *Ghosts of the Tsunami: Death and Life in Japan's Disaster Zone* (London: Jonathan Cape, 2017).

McCullough, Helen Craig (trans.), *The Tale of the Heike* (Stanford, CA: Stanford University Press, 1988).

——, *Yoshitsune: A Fifteenth Century Japanese Chronicle* (Stanford, CA: Stanford University Press, 1966).

Meech-Pekarik, Julia, *The World of the Meiji Print: Impressions of a New Civilization* (New York: Weatherhill, 1987).

Milton, Giles, *Samurai William: The Adventurer Who Unlocked Japan* (London: Hodder & Stoughton, 2002).

Miner, Earl, *An Introduction to Japanese Court Poetry* (Stanford, CA: Stanford University Press, 1968).

Morris, Ivan, *The Nobility of Failure: Tragic Heroes in the History of Japan* (London: Secker & Warburg, 1975).

——, *The World of the Shining Prince: Court Life in Ancient Japan* (New York: Alfred A. Knopf, 1964).

Murasaki, Lady, *The Tale of Genji*, trans. Arthur Waley (North Clarendon, VT: Tuttle Publishing, 2016).

Ō no Yasumaru, *Nihongi: Chronicles of Japan from the Earliest Times to AD 697*, trans. W. G. Aston (London: Routledge, 2010; first published by Kegan Paul, Trench, Trubner & Co., 1896).

Pilling, David, *Bending Adversity: Japan and the Art of Survival* (London: Allen Lane, 2014).

Roberts, John G., *Mitsui: Three Centuries of Japanese Business* (Canada: Weatherhill, 1973).

Sansom, G. B., *Japan: A Short Cultural History* (Tokyo: Charles E. Tuttle Co., 1931).

Satow, E. M., *A Diplomat in Japan* (Berkeley, CA: Stone Bridge Press, 2006; first published by Seeley, Service & Co., 1921).

Screech, Timon, *Tokyo Before Tokyo: Power and Magic in the Shogun's City of Edo* (London: Reaktion Books, 2020).

Seidensticker, Edward, *Low City, High City: Tokyo from Edo to the Earthquake, 1867–1923* (New York: Alfred A. Knopf, 1983).

——, *Tokyo Rising: The City Since the Great Earthquake* (New York: Alfred A. Knopf, 1990).

Seigle, Cecilia Segawa, *Yoshiwara: The Glittering World of the Japanese Courtesan* (Honolulu: University of Hawai'i Press, 1993).

Shiba Ryotaro, *The Last Shogun: The Life of Tokugawa Yoshinobu*, trans. Juliet Winters Carpenter (Tokyo: Kodansha International, 1998).

Stanley, Amy, *Stranger in the Shogun's City, A Woman's Life in Nineteenth Century Japan* (London: Chatto & Windus, 2020).

Steele, M. William, *Alternative Narratives in Modern Japanese History* (London: Routledge, 2003).

Totman, Conrad, *Politics in the Tokugawa Bakufu, 1600–1843* (Boston: Harvard University Press, 1967).

——, *Collapse of the Tokugawa Bakufu, 1862–1868* (Honolulu: University of Hawai'i Press, 2022).

Turnbull, Stephen, *The Book of the Samurai: The Warrior Class of Japan* (London: Bison Books, 1982).

——, *Samurai Women 1184–1877* (Oxford, UK: Osprey Publishing, 2010).

Tyler, Royall (trans.), *The Tale of Genji* (New York: Penguin, 2001); *The Tale of the Heike* (New York: Penguin, 2014).

Varley, H. Paul, *Japanese Culture* (Tokyo: Charles E. Tuttle Co., 1984).

Waley, Arthur, *The Nō Plays of Japan* (Tokyo: Charles E. Tuttle Co., 1921).

Whiting, Robert, *Tokyo Junkie: 60 Years of Bright Lights and Back Alleys . . . and Baseball* (Berkeley, CA: Stone Bridge Press, 2021).

Whitney Hall, John, *Japan in the Muromachi Age* (Ithaca, NY: Cornell University Press, 2010).

Wiley, Peter Booth, with Ichiro Korogi, *Yankees in the Land of the Gods: Commodore Perry and the Opening of Japan* (New York: Viking, 1990).

Wolferen, Karel van, *The Enigma of Japanese Power* (New York: Macmillan, 1989).

Yoshikawa, Eiji, *Taiko: An Epic Novel of War and Glory in Feudal Japan*, trans. William Scott Wilson (Tokyo: Kodansha International, 1992).

Image Credits

p. 6: Exhibition at the Sainsbury Institute of the British Museum. Photograph by Morio. Image via Wikimedia Commons.

p. 8: Photograph by Bigjap. Image via Wikimedia Commons.

p. 12: Photograph by Bariston. Image via Wikimedia Commons.

p. 18: Photograph by Fg2. Image via Wikimedia Commons.

p. 21: Collection of Tokyo National Museum. Image via Wikimedia Commons.

p. 22: Copyright © National Land Image Information (Color Aerial Photographs), Ministry of Land, Infrastructure, Transport and Tourism. Image via Wikimedia Commons.

p. 27: Photograph by 663highland. Image via Wikimedia Commons.

p. 39: Photograph by Fg2. Image via Wikimedia Commons.

p. 42: Collection of University of Michigan Museum of Art. Purchase made possible by the Margaret Watson Parker Art Collection Fund, 1969/2.21.

p. 49: Collection of Enryaku-ji, Mount Hiei. Image from 天皇一二四代 (*Tennōhyakunijūyondai*; "The Japanese Book"), in Bessatsu-Taiyo, Heibonsha, 1988. Image via Wikimedia Commons.

p. 59: Artwork by Tosa Mitsuoki, c. 1600-1700. Image via Wikimedia Commons.

p. 60: Unknown artist, c. 1130. Collection of Tokugawa Art Museum, Nagoya, Japan, 1937. Image via Wikimedia Commons.

p. 64: Photo by Martin Falbisoner. Image via Wikimedia Commons.

p. 69: Collection of Jingo-ji temple, Kyoto. Image via Wikimedia Commons.

p. 70: Unknown artist, c. 1200. Image via Wikimedia Commons.

p. 80: Artwork by Takezaki Suenaga, c. 1293. Image via Wikimedia Commons.

p. 86: Collection of Kyoto Asney Archive. Image via Wikimedia Commons.

p. 89: Collection of the Tokyo National Museum, Tokyo. Photograph by Daderot. Image via Wikimedia Commons.

p. 95: Sesshū Tōyō, *Winter Landscape*, c. 1420–1506. Collection of National Institutes for Cultural Heritage. Image via Emuseum/Wikimedia Commons.

p. 99: Giovanni Nicolao, Nobunaga, c. 1582. Collection of Sanpoji Temple, Tendo City. Image via Wikimedia Commons; Kanō Sōshū, "Imagined portrait of Oda Nobunaga," 1583. Collection of Chōkō-ji (長興寺), Toyota, Aichi, Japan. Image via Wikimedia Commons.

p. 104: Photograph by japan_photo. Image via ebay.com.

p. 107: Unknown artist, c. 1600. Image via Wikimedia Commons.

p. 114: Unknown artist, *Edo zu* ("View of Edo"), pair of six-panel folding screens (detail), c. 1600–1700. Collection of National Museum of Japanese History. Image via Wikimedia Commons.

p. 119: Collection of Tokugawa Art Museum. Image via Wikimedia Commons.

p. 123: Hishikawa Moronobu, *Two Lovers*, c. 1675–80. Image via Met Museum.

p. 130: Toyokuni Utagawa, *Yoru No Fukagawa Geisha*, 1828. Collection of Library of Congress. Image via Wikimedia Commons.

p. 132: Unknown artist, woodblock print, c. 1854. Image via Alamy Stock Photo.

p. 140: Frederick Sutton Studio, *The Last Shogun, 1867. Photograph from Terry Bennett's, Photography in Japan 1853–1912*, p. 107. Image via Wikimedia Commons.

p. 141: Uchida Kuichi, *The Meiji Emperor, 1872, published in Meiji Tenno Gyoden, Kaneo Bun'endo*, Tokyo, 1912. Image via Wikimedia Commons.

p. 147: "Opening of the First Railway in Japan: Arrival of the Mikado," *Illustrated London News*, December 21, 1872. Image via chaari. wordpress.

p. 148: Utagawa Kuniteru, *Tōkyō takanawa tetsudō jōkisha sōkō no zu* ("Illustration of a Steam Locomotive Running on the Takanawa Railroad in Tokyo"), c. 1873. Image courtesy of Met Museum.

p. 150: Unknown photographer, c. 1872. Image via Wikimedia Commons.

p. 157: Artwork by Ōkura Kōtō, January 12, 1894. Japan Centre for Asian Historical Records and the British Library. Image via Wikimedia Commons.

p. 170: Photograph by MeijiShowa. Image via Alamy Stock Photo.

p. 172: M. Nakajima, *Ryounkaku at Asakusa Park*, c. 1897–1922. Collection of Brittingham Family Lantern Slide Collection, University of Wisconsin- Madison Archives.

p. 185: Gaetano Faillace, *Emperor Hirohito and General MacArthur*, September 27, 1945. Collection of United States Army. Image via Wikimedia Commons.

p. 193: Unknown photographer for *Asahi Shimbun*, October 10, 1964. Collection of Government of Japan. Image via Wikimedia Commons.

p. 195: Collection of Dutch National Archives. Image via Wikimedia Commons.

p. 198: Photograph by Newscom. Image via Alamy Stock Photo.

p. 206: Photograph by Matthew Cavanaugh/EPA. Image via Shutterstock.

p. 210: Photograph by Newscom. Image via Alamy Stock Photo.

p. 214: 外務省. Image via Wikimedia Commons.

p. 225: Artwork by Delcarmat. Image via Shutterstock.

Acknowledgments

This book is the culmination of more than forty years of living my life in and around Japan. I'd like to thank the many friends who have been part of that life and the Japan experts whose work I've consulted over the years.

I'm hugely grateful to Pico Iyer, who suggested to Black Inc. that I might be the person to write this book and who set this whole project in motion, and to Peter Barakan, who read parts of the last chapters and made valuable on-the-spot suggestions.

Many thanks to Black Inc. for giving me the chance to pull together all my thoughts of and love of Japan and its history and to tell these wonderful stories. My publisher, Sophy Williams, and my editor, Denise O'Dea, and their team, have been very supportive and receptive of my many demands. In the United States, I'm grateful to Matthew Lore and Anna Bliss and their team at The Experiment, and in England to Ben Yarde-Buller and Kieron Connolly and their team at OldStreet Publishing.

I'd like to acknowledge the scholars whose brilliant work I've used to research this book; the main sources are listed in the bibliography, including the wonderful diaries written by early visitors to Japan. Many thanks to the scholars I've been fortunate enough to have met and consulted over the years and who have generously shared their knowledge with me—Donald Keene, Conrad Totman, and many others.

I'd also like to acknowledge the wonderful resources available in London. While writing this book, I went regularly to the British Museum, to enjoy firstly the Jōmon pots and, as I proceeded through the centuries, to immerse myself in the relevant sections and imagine myself back in old Japan.

I owe a debt of gratitude to Nicolas Wolfers, now Nicolas Maclean, who created the Wolfers Scheme, which later transmogrified into the JET (Japan Exchange and Teaching) Programme. I went to Japan on the very first year of the scheme. Without that marvelous opportunity, my whole life would have been different.

Lastly, bottomless thanks to my husband, Arthur, who as always traveled through the centuries with me. He read every version of every chapter and made very insightful comments. He has lived with this book patiently for the last three years and now knows Oda Nobunaga and everyone else almost as well as I do.

Index

Page numbers in *italics* reference illustrations, maps, and photographs.

About the Author

LESLEY DOWNER is a Japan expert, author, journalist, and historian. She has written four novels, The Shogun Quartet, and several works of nonfiction, including the immersive work of journalism *Women of the Pleasure Quarters: The Secret History of the Geisha* and *The Brothers: The Hidden World of Japan's Richest Family*, which was chosen as a *New York Times* Book of the Year. She has traveled widely and given lectures at the Japan Society New York, at Asia and Japan Societies across the United States, at the Royal Geographic Society and the British Museum in London, and many other venues. She was the historical consultant for Northern Ballet's spectacular 2020 ballet *Geisha* and she appears on *Age of the Samurai: Battle for Japan* (Netflix). She lives in London with her husband, the author Arthur I. Miller.

lesleydowner.com | @lesleydowner

Also available in the Shortest History series

Trade Paperback Originals • $16.95 US | $21.95 CAN

978-1-61519-569-5

978-1-61519-820-7

978-1-61519-814-6

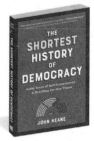

978-1-61519-896-2

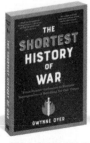

978-1-61519-930-3

978-1-61519-914-3

978-1-61519-948-8

978-1-61519-950-1

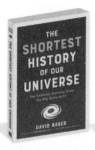

978-1-61519-973-0

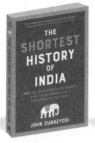

978-1-61519-997-6

978-1-891011-34-4

978-1-891011-45-0